Please Please Me

Tom Wright

methuen | drama

LONDON · NEW YORK · OXFORD · NEW DELHI · SYDNEY

METHUEN DRAMA

Bloomsbury Publishing Plc, 50 Bedford Square, London, WC1B 3DP, UK
Bloomsbury Publishing Inc, 1359 Broadway, New York, NY 10018, USA
Bloomsbury Publishing Ireland, 29 Earlsfort Terrace, Dublin 2,
D02 AY28, Ireland

BLOOMSBURY, METHUEN DRAMA and the Methuen
Drama logo are trademarks of Bloomsbury Publishing Plc.

First published in Great Britain 2026

For legal purposes the Acknowledgements on p. vii
constitute an extension of this copyright page.

Cover design by Muse

Photography by Seamus Ryan

A catalogue record for this book is available from the British Library.

A catalog record for this book is available from the Library of Congress.

ISBN: PB: 978-1-3506-4148-8
ePDF: 978-1-3506-4149-5
eBook: 978-1-3506-4151-8

Series: Modern Plays

Typeset by Mark Heslington Ltd, Scarborough, North Yorkshire
Printed and bound in Great Britain

For product safety related questions contact
productsafety@bloomsbury.com.

To find out more about our authors and books visit
www.bloomsbury.com and sign up for our newsletters.

Kiln Theatre presents

Please Please Me

Written by Tom Wright
Directed by Amit Sharma

Cast

Brian	**Calam Lynch**
John	**Noah Ritter**
Peter/Mike/Dizz	**William Robinson**
Geoffrey/Harry/Derek	**Arthur Wilson**
Cynthia/Cilla/Aunt Mimi	**Eleanor Worthington-Cox**

Creative Team

Writer	**Tom Wright**
Director	**Amit Sharma**
Set and Co-Costume Designer	**Tom Piper**
Co-Costume Designer	**Deborah Andrews**
Lighting Designer	**Rory Beaton**
Composer and Sound Designer	**David Shrubsole**
Movement Director	**Jess Williams**
Casting Director	**Amy Ball CDG**
Voice and Dialect Coach	**Mary Howland**
Fight and Intimacy Director	**Bethan Clark**
Associate Sound Designer and Production Sound Engineer	**Chris Simpson**
Associate Fight and Intimacy Director	**Robin Hellier**
Assistant Director	**Hetty Hodgson**
Wigs, Hair and Make-Up Supervisor	**Sharon Pearson**

Production Team

Production Manager	**Pam Nichol**
Deputy Production Manager	**Muriel de Palma**
Company Stage Manager	**Lois Sime**
Deputy Stage Manager	**Caroline Meer**
Assistant Stage Manager (Book Cover)	**Odette Robertson**
Technician	**Anna LeClair**
Wardrobe Manager	**Charlotte Jade Murray**

Wigs, Hair and Make-Up Manager	**Milica Rosellini**
Stage Crew	**Emily Huxley**
Tech Swing	**Fabian Pilon**
Production Carpenter	**Calum Walker**
Rehearsal Carpenter	**Ally Friedman**
Production Rigger	**Jess Wilson**
Production Electrician	**Paul Salmon**
Lighting Programmer	**Stephen Settle**
Set Build by	**Liverpool Scenic**
Sound supplied by	**Autograph**
Furniture supplied by	**Propworks**
Lighting supplied by	**Sparks Theatrical Hire**

Thanks to Paul Anderson for continued support on productions.

Special thanks to Hampstead Theatre and Tara Theatre.

Please Please Me is generously supported by Cockayne Grants for the Arts, a donor advised fund held at Prism, the Gift Fund.

COCKAYNE

We are also grateful to The Golsoncott Foundation for supporting this production.

Cast

Calam Lynch
Brian

For Kiln Theatre: *Wife*.

Calam Lynch recently wrapped shooting a series lead, Sam, in *Ride or Die* for Amazon, opposite Octavia Spencer and Hannah Waddingham. He can now be seen in the See-Saw Films project for Sky/Starz *Sweetpea*, as well as *What It Feels Like for a Girl* for Hera Pictures and the BBC.

Theatre credits include: Oswald in Ibsen's *Ghosts* (Abbey, Dublin).

Film and TV credits include: *Miss Austen* with Keeley Hawes, S2 of *Lord of the Rings* and *Archie* directed by Paul Andrew Williams, in which he plays the younger title role of Cary Grant, with Jason Isaacs as the elder. Other highlights include: Terence Davies' feature film *Benediction* with Jack Lowden, Theo Sharpe in *Bridgerton* S2, Disney feature film *Black Beauty*, BBC drama *Mrs Wilson* with Ruth Wilson and *Derry Girls*.

Noah Ritter
John

Noah Ritter is a performer, making his professional stage debut at Kiln.

Film and TV include: *Running Man* (Paramount Pictures), as well as four other soon to be released credits for Amazon and Netflix.

William Robinson
Peter/Mike/Dizz

William Robinson graduated from LAMDA before starring in multi-award-winning two-hander *Bacon*. Following the show's initial success, he reprised his role for a summer Tour including the Edinburgh Fringe. *Bacon* was then selected as part of the Fringe Encore Series and played in the Soho Playhouse in NYC throughout January 2024.

William played the lead Nero in *Britannicus* at the Lyric Hammersmith, for which he was awarded second prize at the Ian Charleson Awards in 2023. He went on to star as Mark Antony in the RSC's *Julius Caesar,* and in the Globe's production of *All's Well That Ends Well.* Most recently, William starred as Cosmo in *The Pitchfork Disney* at the King's Head Theatre.

Film and TV credits include: *Bohnhoeffer, Masters of the Air* and *The Silence and the Noise.*

Arthur Wilson
Geoffrey/Harry/Derek

Theatre credits include: *Here There Are Blueberries* (Tetonic Theatre/Stratford East); *Much Ado About Nothing* (RSC); *Mnemonic* (Complicité/National Theatre); *First Touch* (Nottingham Playhouse); *Force Majeure* (Donmar Warehouse); *She Ventures and He Wins* (Young Vic); *Genesis Inc.* (Hampstead Theatre); *Man and Superman* (National Theatre); *Things I Know to Be True* (Frantic Assembly); *The Tempest* (AFTLS); *Persuasion* (Royal Exchange); *Richard II* (Shakespeare's Globe); *Twelfth Night, The Taming of the Shrew, A Midsummer Night's Dream, The Comedy of Errors* (Propeller Theatre); *Hard Times, If I Were You, Tom's Midnight Garden* (Library Theatre) and *A Hole in the Fence* (Box of Tricks).

TV credits include: *D-DAY: The Unheard Tapes, Casualty, Call the Midwife, Law and Order* and *Sea of Souls.*

Film credits include: *The Victoria Project* and *Opus.*

Eleanor Worthington-Cox
Cynthia/Cilla/Aunt Mimi

Theatre credits includes: *Mary Page Marlowe* (Old Vic); *Much Ado About Nothing* (RSC); *The Little Foxes* (Young Vic); *Next to Normal* (Donmar Warehouse/Wyndham's); *The Secret Life of Bees* (Almeida); *Jerusalem* (Apollo); *Tom Cat* (Southwark Playhouse); *Bugsy Malone* (Lyric Hammersmith); *To Kill a Mockingbird* (Regent's Park Open Air Theatre) and *Matilda: The Musical* (Cambridge Theatre – Olivier Award for Best Actress in a Musical).

TV credits include: *Britannia*, *The Irregulars*, *The Enfield-Haunting*, *Cucumber* and *Hetty Feather*.

Film credits include: *About a Bell*, *Gwen*, *Action Point* and *Maleficent*.

Creative Team

Tom Wright
Writer

Tom Wright is a writer, director and dramaturg for theatre and film. He is currently the Artistic Director at Leeds Playhouse.

Tom's two back-to-back debut plays *My Dad's Gap Year* (Park Theatre) and *Undetectable* (King's Head Theatre) achieved acclaim with seven Off West End Award nominations, including Best New Play and Most Promising Playwright. *Undetectable* returned the following year and has since been licensed worldwide. Tom's third play *Very Special Guest Star* (Omnibus Theatre) earned praise from The Guardian as a 'thoroughly original play that entertains, provokes and unsettles'.

Returning to his hometown of Coventry, Tom premiered *I Ain't Dumb* at the Belgrade Theatre as part of UK City of Culture celebrations. Additional projects include *Rebel Song* (The Other Palace), a musical adaptation of Jamie O'Neill's award-winning novel *At Swim, Two Boys*, and *Sirens* and *White Lies* (ArtsEd) a double-bill of new plays that he both wrote and directed.

As a theatre director, Tom's recent credits include *Dumbledore Is So Gay* (Southwark Playhouse, Pleasance Theatre and Vault Festival – Origins Award Winner), *Blowhole* (Soho Theatre and Pleasance Theatre) and *Tumble Tuck* (King's Head Theatre and Underbelly Edinburgh). Tom has been Associate Director to Rikki Beadle-Blair and Indhu Rubasingham on various productions including Indhu's Olivier Award nominated production of *The Invisible Hand* (Kiln Theatre).

Tom's award-winning debut short film *Stockholm* premiered at BFI Flare: London LGBTQ+ Film Festival, garnering recognition at festivals internationally and winning Best Cinematography at the LA LGBTQ+ Festival. The film has amassed over 100k views online. His second short film *Kweenship* was completed in the same year, followed by a commission from Sky Arts to make his third short film *Sent To Cov* for national broadcast. The film was subsequently shortlisted for a Broadcast Digital Award.

In his previous role as Associate Artistic Director at Kiln Theatre, Tom worked closely with Artistic Directors Indhu Rubasingham and Amit Sharma on commissioning, developing, and programming new work, including contributions from acclaimed writers such as Marina Carr, Zadie Smith, and Ryan Calais Cameron, with productions successfully transferring to the Abbey Theatre (Dublin), Brooklyn Academy of Music (New York), and London's West End. Tom also founded the Kiln's Listen Local Writers Programmes, empowering first-time local writers to share their voices.

As Head of Artist Development at The Old Vic, Tom steered the prestigious Old Vic 12 initiative to success over five years, culminating in a ground-breaking repertory season – cut short only by the pandemic. Through this and a range of innovative projects, Tom nurtured over fifteen new plays and propelled countless theatre artists into the next stages of their careers, many of whom are fast becoming major names.

Tom is a trustee of the Olivier Award winning Papatango Theatre Company, as well having participated in the Programming Committee for the Belgrade Theatre. He is a sector leader in LGBTQ+ inclusion, conducting bespoke training workshops, whilst dedicating himself to broadening and diversifying the LGBTQ+ cannon.

Self-organisation, mentorship and skill sharing are central to Tom's collaborative activity. Whether offering feedback on scripts, facilitating workshops, running playwriting courses, or curating shadowing placements, Tom hopes this nurturing of the next generation of talent forms an ever-expanding revolution of empowered, joyful and disruptive theatre artists.

Amit Sharma
Director

Amit Sharma is Artistic Director of Kiln Theatre where he directed *The Purists*, *Pins and Needles* and the critically acclaimed sell-out run of *Retrograde*. Before joining the Kiln Theatre as Associate Director, he was previously Deputy Artistic Director of Birmingham Rep, Associate Artistic Director at the Royal Exchange, Manchester, and Associate Director at Graeae Theatre Company where his journey into theatre began.

Sharma has directed two productions at the National Theatre – *The Solid Life of Sugar Water* (Graeae Theatre Company/Theatre Royal Plymouth co-production) and *The Boy with Two Hearts* (also Wales Millennium Centre). He also co-directed *Prometheus Awakes*, one of the largest outdoor productions featuring Deaf and disabled artists as part of the London 2012 Cultural Olympiad (Graeae Theatre Company/Greenwich + Docklands International Festival/ Stockton International Riverside Festival/La Fura Dels Baus), and *Aruna and the Raging Sun* in Chennai, India as part of UK/India Year of Culture 2017.

He is an international award-winning director of theatre and television. Sharma is a BAFTA-nominated director for his two films which were part of the *Criptales* season on BBC and BBC America. He also co-directed the award-winning BBC and Netflix television drama *Then Barbara Met Alan* (Best Single Drama, 2023 Broadcast Awards). He began his training at Graeae Theatre Company with *Missing Piece 1*.

His other theatre credits include: *One Under* (Graeae Theatre Company/Theatre Royal Plymouth); *Cosmic Scallies* (Graeae Theatre Company/Royal Exchange) and *Iron Man*

(Graeae Theatre Company/international Tour). His other television work includes *Hamish* and *Thunderbox*.

Tom Piper
Set and Co-Costume Designer

For Kiln Theatre/Tricycle: *The Purists, Girl on an Altar, White Teeth, The Wolf with Snakeskin Shoes, The House that Will Not Stand* and *Red Velvet*.

Other theatre credits include: *The Duchess (of Malfi)* (Trafalgar/Lyceum, Edinburgh); *The Scent of Roses, Rhinoceros, Mrs Puntila, Hay Fever* (Lyceum, Edinburgh); *Macbeth (an undoing)* (Lyceum Theatre, Edinburgh/Rose Theatre/Theatre fora New Audience – Scottish Critics' Awards for Best Design); *Jesus Trilogy* (Dublin Theatre Festival); *Never Let Me Go* (Rose Theatre/Bristol Old Vic/Malvern Theatres/Northampton Theatre/UK Tour); over fifty productions for The RSC, most recently *Faith, The Box of Delights, Hamnet, The Tempest* (RSC); *Medea* (National Theatre of Scotland/Edinburgh International Festival); *Cyrano de Bergerac* (National Theatre of Scotland); *Small Acts of Love, Endgame, King Lear, Hamlet, The Libertine, Nora* (Citizens Theatre); *Apex Predator, iHo, The Haystack, King of Hells Palace* (Hampstead Theatre); *The Cherry Orchard, Les Liaisons Dangereuses* (Bristol Old Vic); *The Great Wave, The Birthday Party, Blinded by the Sun* and *Oh What a Lovely War* (Royal National Theatre).

Opera credits include: *A Midsummer Night's Dream* (Scottish Opera); *Orfeo* (ROH/Roundhouse); *Queen of Spades, Rusalka, Eugene Onegin* and *Don Giovanni* (Garsington Opera).

Other work includes: *Blood Swept Lands and Seas of Red* at the Tower of London for which he received an MBE for services to theatre and First World War commemorations. He has won an Olivier Award for Best Costume Design for *The Histories* (RSC) and Scottish Critics' Award for Best Design for *Twelfth Night* (Dundee Rep) and *Macbeth (an undoing)*.

Deborah Andrews

Co-Costume Designer

Deborah Andrews studied Fashion Design at Central Saint Martins College of Art and then worked in fashion before being lured into the theatre. She has worked as a costume designer, associate costume designer and costume supervisor in both opera and theatre.

Costume designer credits include: *The Comedy about Spies* (Noël Coward Theatre); *House of Games* (Hampstead Theatre); *The Promise* (Chichester Festival Theatre); *Henry IV* (Donmar Warehouse/St. Ann's Warehouse, New York) and *The Glass Piano* (The Coronet).

Co-costume designer credits include: *Guys and Dolls* (Bridge Theatre) and *Patriots* (Almeida/Noël Coward Theatre/Ethel Barrymore Theatre, New York).

Associate costume designer credits include: *Oh Mary!* (Trafalgar Theatre); *The Doctor* (Almeida); *The Birthday Party* (Harold Pinter Theatre); *The Shark Is Broken* (Ambassadors Theatre/UK Tour) and *Sunny Afternoon* (UK Tour).

Costume supervisor theatre credits include: *Dance of Death* (Orange Tree Theatre); *Inter Alia* (National Theatre/ Wyndham's Theatre); *Angels in America* (National Theatre/ Neil Simon Theatre, New York); *Oslo, Peter Gynt, The Welkin, Afterlife, London Tide* (National Theatre); *To Kill a Mockingbird* (Wyndham's Theatre/UK Tour); *Elektra* (Theatre Royal Brighton/Duke of York's Theatre); *Spring Awakening, Filumena, Medea, Ink, The Twilight Zone* (Almeida); *Prima Facie, The Birthday Party* (Harold Pinter Theatre); *Company* (Gielgud Theatre); *As You Desire Me* (Playhouse Theatre); *Double Feature, Good People, Wonderland, Hapgood* (Hampstead Theatre); *Sunny Afternoon* (Hampstead Theatre/ Harold Pinter/UK Tour); *King Lear, The Winslow Boy* (Chichester Festival Theatre); *Shakespeare Trilogy, Closer, Philadelphia* and *Here I Come!* (Donmar Warehouse).

Costume supervisor opera credits include: *Otello, Oklahoma, Werther, Katya Kabanova* (Grange Park Opera); *Maria Luisa, Vanessa, The Rape of Lucretia, La Bohème, St Matthew Passion* (Glyndebourne); *Agrippina, Orfeo, Salome, Alcina, Child of Our Time, Trojans, Ernani, The Mikado, Don Giovanni* (ENO/Basel/Oslo) and *Cosi fan tutte* (ENO/Barbican).

Rory Beaton
Lighting Designer

Rory Beaton is a two-time BroadwayWorld Award winner. He was awarded Best Lighting Design for his work on both *Jesus Christ Superstar* and *The Lord of the Rings*. His work on the West End musical *The Time Traveller's Wife* also earned him a WhatsOnStage Award nomination.

For Kiln Theatre: *Pins and Needles*.

West End credits include: *Burlesque: The Musical* (Savoy Theatre); *The Time Traveller's Wife* (Apollo Theatre); *For Black Boys …* (Garrick Theatre/Apollo Theatre); *Death Drop: Back in the Habit, Instructions for a Teenage Armageddon* (Garrick Theatre); *Your Lie in April* (Harold Pinter Theatre); *Wild About You* (Theatre Royal Drury Lane); *The Merchant of Venice 1936* (Criterion Theatre/Trafalgar Theatre); *I Love You, You're Perfect, Now Change!* (London Coliseum) and *Jo: The Little Women Musical* (Theatre Royal Drury Lane).

Other theatre credits include: *Sweeney Todd* (Birmingham Rep); *Disney's High School Musical* (Lowry); *The Merchant of Venice 1936* (Royal Shakespeare Company); *Charlie and the Chocolate Factory* (Global Tour); *Midnight: A New Musical* (Sadler's Wells East); *The Lord of the Rings* (Chicago/New Zealand/Australia/Singapore/UK); *Jesus Christ Superstar* (Watermill); *Summer Holiday* (Sheffield Crucible); *Tom Fletcher's The Creakers* (Southbank/Theatre Royal Plymouth); *Little Shop of Horrors* (Hope Mill Theatre/Liverpool Playhouse); *Military Wives: The Musical* (York Theatre Royal); *Death of a Salesman* (UK Tour); *For Black Boys …, Jews. In*

Their Own Words (Royal Court Theatre); *Lovely Ugly City* (Almeida); *The Jungle Book* (Chichester Festival Theatre); *Principles of Deception*, *Top G's Like Me* (Royal & Derngate); *Unexpected Twist* (UK Tour); *The Mountaintop* (UK Tour); *Midsummer* (Mercury) and *Spike* (UK Tour).

David Shrubsole
Composer and Sound Designer

David Shrubsole studied music at Trinity College of Music, and dramaturgy and critical theory at Goldsmiths University.

For Kiln Theatre: *The Ballad of Hattie and James*, *Wife*, *Holy Sh!t*.

Theatre credits include: *Dear Octopus*, *The Great Wave*, *My Country: a Work in Progress*, *The Threepenny Opera*, *Table*, *London Road*, *The Magistrate*, *She Stoops to Conquer*, *Major Barbara*, *The Enchantment*, *The Alchemist*, *My Fair Lady* (National Theatre); *Charlie and the Chocolate Factory*, *Sweeney Todd*, *Sunshine on Leith*, *The Crucible*, *Europe*, *Dr Korczak's Example*, *Annie*, *Peter Pan*, *Martin Guerre* (Leeds Playhouse); *American Psycho* (Almeida); *The Great Wall* (Singapore Drama Centre); *Porgy and Bess*, *Romeo and Juliet*, *Hello Dolly*, *Much Ado About Nothing* (Regent's Park Open Air Theatre); *A Chorus Line*, *Assassins*, *Ain't Misbehavin'*, *Amadeus* (Sheffield Crucible); *Conversations with Coward*, *Just So*, *Hayfever* (Chichester Festival Theatre); *Of Mice and Men* (Mercury); *Hobson's Choice* (Watermill Theatre); *Total Eclipse* (Menier Chocolate Factory); *You Are Here* (Goodspeed Opera House); *Something Wicked This Way Comes* (Delaware Theatre Company); *The Three Musketeers*, *Troilus and Cressida* (Chicago Shakespeare); *Gaslight* (Old Vic); *A Streetcar Named Desire* (Theatr Clwyd/Leicester Curve); *Miss Saigon* (Prince Edward Theatre); *The Wind in the Willows* (London Palladium) and *Epitaph for George Dillon* (Comedy). He was awarded the 2017 Drama Desk Award for Outstanding Revue for his work *Life Is for Living: Conversations with Coward*.

Jess Williams
Movement Director

Jess Williams was trained at the London Contemporary Dance School and the Laban Centre.

As movement director or choreographer, theatre credits include: *Nye* (National Theatre); *Hamlet Hail to the Thief* (RSC/Factory International); *Lost and Found* (Factory International/Aviva Studios); *Our Town* (Welsh National Theatre); *Richard III* (Shakespeare's Globe); *The Boy with Two Hearts* (Wales Millennium Centre/National Theatre); *Poor* (Gate Theatre, Dublin); *Snake in the Grass, Rope, Cinderella, Mother Goose, Celebrated Virgins* (Theatr Clwyd); *Hair* (Konzert und Theater St. Gallen); *Byth Bythoedd Amen, Merched Caerdydd* (Theatr Cymru); *A Little Piece of You* (Theatre Royal Drury Lane); *Around the World in 80 Days* (Theatre by the Lake), *Blood Harmony, Petrichor* (ThickSkin); *A Walk Is Not Just a Walk* (Lyric Theatre, Belfast) and *Constellations* (National Centre for Performing Arts, Mumbai).

As associate director or associate movement director, theatre credits include: *I Think We Are Alone, The Unreturning, The Curious Incident of the Dog in the Night-Time* (Frantic Assembly); *The Ocean at the End of the Lane, Beginning* (National Theatre) and *Dracula: Mina's Reckoning* (National Theatre of Scotland).

Amy Ball CDG
Casting Director

Recent theatre credits includes: *1536, Romans, Cold War, Christmas Day, A Doll's House, Daddy* (Almeida); *The Weir, The Years, The Hills of California, Good, Uncle Vanya* (Harold Pinter Theatre); *Small Hotel* (Theatre Royal Bath); *Mrs Warren's Profession, Hamnet, Unicorns* (Garrick Theatre); *The Hunger Games* (Troubadour Canary Wharf Theatre); *Slave Play* (Noël Coward Theatre); *Jerusalem* (Apollo) and *Leopoldstadt* (Wyndham's Theatre).

Mary Howland
Voice and Dialect Coach

Mary Howland studied for her MA in Voice Studies at the Central School of Speech and Drama in 1999, and worked as a voice and speech teacher at schools including RADA, Central and LAMDA.

She has provided accent coaching for theatre companies including the Royal Court, Birmingham Rep, the Bush Theatre, Mischief Theatre and the Donmar Warehouse.

Theatre credits include: *Standing at the Sky's Edge* (Crucible); *Top Girls*, *Lieutenant of Inishmore* (Liverpool Everyman); *An Octoroon* (National Theatre); *Our Country's Good* (Out of Joint); *Much Ado About Nothing*, *The Mysteries* (Shakespeare's Globe) and *Sylvia* (Old Vic).

TV and film credits include: *The Spanish Princess*, *Behind Her Eyes*, *Murdered by My Boyfriend* (Georgina Campbell – Best Actress Bafta, 2015), *The Rising*, *Ridley Road*, *The Young Woman and the Sea*, *This Town*, *How to Have Sex*, *Rivals*, *I Swear* (Robert Aramayo – Best Actor Bafta, 2026) and *Prisoner 951*.

Bethan Clark
Fight and Intimacy Director

For Kiln Theatre: *The Ministry of Lesbian Affairs*.

Theatre credits include: *Driftwood, Cyrano de Bergerac, Cowbois, Romeo and Juliet* (RSC); *A Midsummer Night's Dream* (RSC/Unicorn Theatre), *Marvin's Binoculars, The Bolds* (Unicorn Theatre); *The Merry Wives of Windsor, Princess Essex, Romeo and Juliet* (Shakespeare's Globe); *Marie & Rosetta* (Rose Theatre/Chichester Festival Theatre/@SohoPlace); *Lord of the Flies, Coram Boy, A Midsummer Night's Dream, Cinderella* (Chichester Festival Theatre); *Summerfolk, End, The Hot Wing King, Odyssey: The Underworld, Dixon and Daughters* (National Theatre); *Inside No. 9: Stage/Fright* (Wyndham's Theatre/UK

Tour); *Dracula, Ghosts, Our Country's Good, Wedding Band*
(Lyric Hammersmith); *ROAD, Liberation* (Royal Exchange);
Crown of Blood, A Streetcar Named Desire (Crucible); *Red Rogue
of Bala, Lord of the Flies, Mold Riots, Thick as Thieves* (Theatr
Clywd); *Calamity Jane* (UK Tour); *Twelfth Night* (Not Too
Tame/Shakespeare North Playhouse); *Othello* (Liverpool
Everyman); *The Swell* (Orange Tree Theatre); *Brassed Off, A
Little Princess* (Theatre by the Lake); *Wendy: A Peter Pan Story*
(Theatre Royal Bath); *Hello and Goodbye, A View from the
Bridge, Everything Is Possible: The York Suffragettes* (York
Theatre Royal); *The Prince* (Southwark Playhouse); *As You
Like It* (Northern Broadsides); *The Last Ship* (Northern Stage/
UK Tour): *Macbeth* (Queen's Theatre, Hornchurch/Derby)
and *The Hired Man* (Queen's Theatre, Hornchurch/Hull
Truck/Oldham Coliseum).

Chris Simpson

Associate Sound Designer and Production Sound Engineer

Chris Simpson trained at Guildhall School of Music and
Drama.

As sound designer, credits includes: *Spring Awakening* (Royal
Academy of Music); *Spring Awakening* (Drama Centre,
Singapore); *Hamlet! The Musical* (UK Tour); *Pericles* (Regent's
Park Open Air Theatre); *Rent* (Victoria Theatre, Singapore)
and *Tommy* (Royal Academy of Music).

As associate sound designer, credits include: *Operation
Mincemeat* (Fortune Theatre/UK Tour); *Charlie and the
Chocolate Factory* (UK Tour); *She Loves Me, Guys and Dolls*
(Crucible, Sheffield); *Forbidden City* (Esplanade, Singapore);
Our Ladies of Perpetual Succour (Duke of York's Theatre);
Rent (St James Theatre/UK Tour); *The Last Mermaid* (Weston
Studio, Cardiff); *Oh! What a Lovely War* (Theatre Royal
Stratford East); *Dear World* (Charing Cross); *Crazy for You*
(Novello Theatre); *Aspects of Love* (UK Tour); *Jerry Springer –
The Opera* (London/UK Tour); *Peter Pan* (West Yorkshire
Playhouse); *Change & Eng* (Kuala Lumpur) and *Chicago*
(Kuala Lumpur).

Hetty Hodgson
Assistant Director

Hetty Hodgson is a theatre director who makes work which is both political and playful. She is the Artistic Director of multi-award winning Pigfoot Theatre and a supported Artist with ThickSkin Theatre who they work regularly with as an Associate. They are an Associate Artist with National Youth Theatre, where she was the Bryan Forbes Trainee Director with the REP Company 2024–25.

YOUR STORIES LIVE HERE

'A marvellous community reality . . . alive with challenge and promise.'
James Baldwin

Kiln Theatre is the creative and cultural hub of Kilburn in Brent, a uniquely diverse area of London where over 140 languages are spoken. We are a place of creative transformation and artistic ambition – an empowering space where community connection sits at the centre of everything we do. From the heart of Kilburn, we stage an internationally acclaimed programme of UK premieres and dynamic revivals – real human stories that entertain, fire the imagination and reflect the world around us.

As Tricycle and now Kiln, we are proud of our artistic history and passionate about our future. We nurture talent and develop pathways whilst celebrating diversity and removing barriers – driving world-class theatre and opening up opportunities for who gets to make it.

'Kiln Theatre has revitalised the cultural life of Brent and brings world-class theatre at an affordable price to people from all walks of life.' Zadie Smith

We believe that theatre can be for anyone, and we are committed to nurturing the talent of young people and providing a platform for their voices to be heard whilst working with older people to create a thriving community around our theatre. A neighbourhood venue shaping national conversation. Our doors are open to all, and your stories live here.

'I wanted to say thank you for creating the most diverse theatre I have been to. In terms of race, culture, class, age, everything – not only in the selection of shows and actors, but in the audience.' Audience member

Kiln Theatre, 269 Kilburn High Road, London, NW6 7JR

KilnTheatre.com | info@KilnTheatre.com

 | @KilnTheatre

CREATIVE ENGAGEMENT AT KILN

We create projects with and for people of all ages who live, learn or work in Brent and North-West London. Our programmes encourage people to have fun, connect, be creative, discover a career or an interest in theatre, and have their voices heard.

LEARNING

We believe all young people should have access to arts and culture, and experience the wider benefits the arts can have on connection and confidence. **Arrive Build Create** (formerly Minding the Gap) has been running for 20 years, working with EAL and ESOL departments in local schools and colleges to provide creative drama-based sessions for newly arrived young people. The project aims to develop creativity, confidence and engagement in the arts. For Brent schools, we run free **Backstage Workshops**, Continuous Professional Development for teachers and **School Residencies**, a bespoke year-long programme designed with local schools to support the Drama curriculum and link to the industry. We also host Teacher Previews and provide free Resource Packs. We deliver **Fullworks**, a week-long half term project which explores careers in theatre, open to students from Brent schools aged 14–15 and **Placements** (in partnership with Further and Higher Education centres).

PARTICIPATION

Our Participation work is rooted in Brent & North-West London and celebrates the unique cultural and artistic life of our local area. The Participation programme covers all work with and for local residents who are interested in engaging in theatre as aspiring artists or audiences, providing opportunities to have fun and socialise, or share stories with neighbours. We aim to listen to and advocate for the priorities, heritages and stories of local residents through co-creation. We host Dementia Friendly film screenings each month and Kiln Masterclasses every quarter, delivered by creatives from Kiln shows and Kiln Community Collaborators; a London Living Wage paid facilitation training programme.

From 2024–26 we've embarked on an ambitious community engaged heritage project. Celebrating Our Stories: the Kilburn High Road Project, celebrates and platforms the hidden stories of the High Road and the residents, artists, businesses and organisations who call Kilburn home. Across the first two years of the project, Kiln has engaged residents of all ages in co-created multi art-form activity, including events, performances and upskilling opportunities delivering 284 workshops and events with and for over 2000 participants. 2026 marks the final year of the project, bringing the programme to a public-facing and exciting conclusion with the Kilburn High Road Festival (eight events across 16 days on the High Road Capturing Kilburn, Sound of Kilburn, Passages, High Road Unframed), an intergenerational production performed by 80 local residents aged 7-91 and Neighbours, an employability upskilling programme. The focus of the festival is on sharing this work publicly, animating spaces along the High Road and inviting wider audiences to experience Kilburn's stories and cultural heritage through theatre, music and visual art. The project has been supported by the Community Advisory Board; 12 key local stakeholders.

This project is made possible with The National Lottery Fund with thanks to National Lottery Players.

GET INVOLVED

To find out more about our work and how to get involved, **scan the QR code**, visit **kilntheatre.com/creative-engagement**, or email us on **getinvolved@kilntheatre.com** for more information about our work and how to get involved.

SUPPORT OUR WORK

Welcome to Kiln Theatre!

We're a proudly local theatre, but our stories travel far – from the heart of Kilburn to the West End and beyond. Our mission is clear: bringing you bold and engaging work that fires the imagination and reflects the world around us.

Each year we must raise £1m to champion diversity on and off stage, inspire the next generation of artists, and ensure that anyone, no matter their background, can access extraordinary theatre. Will you help us?

BECOME A KILN FRIEND

From just £5 per month, you can enjoy:

- Access to Priority Booking

- Exclusive updates and insights from Kiln

- Invitations to special supporters' events

From £50 per month, you can also become a Kiln Friend at Silver or Gold level and access an even wider range of special events.

JOIN THE KILN CIRCLE

Kiln Circle donors sit at the heart of Kiln Theatre, and their support underpins all our work. Join the Circle from £2,500 per year and access exclusive events, Opening Nights, rehearsals and unique opportunities to get close to the work on our stage and the artists who make it.

MAKE A DONATION

Donations of any size are also welcome and help sustain our mission of making theatre for all.

SUPPORT

To join our community of supporters, donate or find out how you can get involved, **scan the QR code**, visit **KilnTheatre.com/give** or call the Fundraising team **on 020 7625 0132**.

Thank you.

Registered Charity No. 276892

THANK YOU

A big thank you to all our supporters. We would not be able to continue our work without the support of the following:

Statutory Funders
Arts Council England
The National Lottery Heritage Fund

Companies
The Agency (London) Ltd
Breathe HR
Skadden, Arps, Slate, Meagher & Flom LLP and Affiliates
Sullivan & Cromwell LLP

Major Donors And Kiln Circle
Nick and Aleksandra Barnes
Primrose and David Bell
Jules and Cheryl Burns
M. Michele Burns and Deborah A. Jamison
Mary and Jim Callaghan
Jim Carter and Imelda Staunton
Chalmers Family Foundation
F Charlwood
Laure Zanchi Duvoisin
Gary and Carol Fethke
The Garcia Family Foundation
Matthew Greenburgh and Helen Payne
Ros and Alan Haigh
Mary Clancy Hatch
Linda Keenan
Adam Kenwright
Jonathan Levy and Gabrielle Rifkind
Brian and Clare Linden
Frances Magee
Patrick and Sarah Ryan

Dame Susie Sainsbury
Jon and NoraLee Sedmak
Dr Miriam Stoppard
Ondine Upton and James Park
Peter Wallace

Gold Friends
Maria de Esteban Belzuz
John and Anne Blood
Ian Chalmers
Henry Chu and James Baer
Sue Fletcher
Frances Lynn
Alison McLean and Michael Farthing
Richard Naylor
Ann and Peter Sprinz

Silver Friends
Pippa Adamson
Louis Charalambous and Debbie Haith
John and Susan Coldstream
James and Catherine Flett-Longeval
Robert and Jeannie Golden
Nicola Horton and Tiffany Evans
Ankit Kumar
Sita McIntosh
Roseline and Dennis Neveling
Sheri and Daryl Orts
Emma Thompson and Greg Wise
Tom Young and Lesley Clough
Steve and Sandar Warshal

Legacy Gifts
Gillian Hooper
Harry Frank Rose

Trusts And Foundations
29th May 1961 Charitable Trust
The Atkin Foundation
Backstage Trust
Bertha Foundation
The Big Give – Arts for Impact
Chapman Charitable Trust'
City Bridge Foundation –
London's biggest independent
charity funder
Cockayne Grants for the Arts, a
donor advised fund held at
Prism, the Gift Fund
Flore Foundation
Gale Charitable Trust

The Golsoncott Foundation
Hollick Family Foundation
The John S Cohen Foundation
John Lyon's Charity
John Thaw Foundation
The Mackintosh Foundation
Maria Björnson Memorial Fund
Marie-Louise von Motesiczky
Charitable Trust
Pears Foundation
The Radcliffe Trust
The Roddick Foundation
Theatre Artists Fund Pilot
Programme
The Vanderbilt Family
Foundation
The Vandervell Foundation
Wembley Stadium Foundation

We are also grateful to all our Kiln Friends, and all those who wish
to remain anonymous.

HIRE OUR SPACES

Conveniently located on the Kilburn High Road, Kiln Theatre is a dynamic building offering a variety of unique spaces for rehearsals, workshops, private events, meetings, auditions, film screenings and celebrations.

KILN THEATRE AUDITORIUM

Our 290-seat capacity Main House is available for one-off, large-scale special events. With two levels, the auditorium offers flexible seating options, and level access and wheelchair accessibility to our stalls level.

REHEARSAL ROOM

With a standing capacity of 70, and 50 seated, our Rehearsal Room offers a bright, open space for rehearsals and workshops. With the adjacent Quiet Room and additional spaces available, the Rehearsal Room is an ideal space to host your rehearsal period.

JAMES BALDWIN STUDIO

An intimate studio space with a flexible capacity of 25–50, the James Baldwin Studio is perfect for smaller-scale rehearsals, auditions and workshops.

SUSIE SAINSBURY FOYER

A quiet and secluded hideaway upstairs in our Circle foyer, the Susie Sainsbury Foyer can host up to 25 standing for drinks receptions.

JOHN LYONS SPACE

Nestled at the heart of Kiln Theatre, the John Lyons Space can be transformed for daytime workshops, to evening receptions and events. With a standing capacity of 70, and 40 seated, its proximity to the Bar area and adjoining foyer space makes it a dynamic and flexible space.

CINEMA

Kiln Cinema boasts an 8-metre screen, 291 seating capacity and state-of-the art audio-visual equipment, making it the perfect space for conferences, birthday parties, film screenings, film shoots and away days.

FIND OUT MORE

To find out more about our spaces or enquire about a hire, **scan the QR**, visit **KilnTheatre.com/our-story/hire/**, or email **hires@ kilntheatre.com** to speak to a member of the team.

FOR KILN THEATRE

Artistic Director
Amit Sharma

Executive Director
Iain Goosey

....

Literary Associate
Sam Potter

Producer
Lisa Cagnacci

Producer (Maternity Cover)
Kate Baiden

**Stage One Bridge The Gap
Trainee Producer**
Anousha Karim

**Assistant to the Artistic & the
Executive Director**
Monica Cox

....

Head of Audiences & Sales
Spyros Kois

Marketing Manager
Susannah Shepherd

Marketing Officer
Tristan Simpson

Press Representative
Jo Allan PR

**Box Office & Ticketing
Manager**
Andrew McCullough

Assistant Box Office Manager
Gee Mumford

Box Office Supervisor
Josh Radcliffe

Box Office Assistants
Faizan Ahmed
Jonah Garrett-Bannister
Anna Lines
Moya Matthews
Jacqueline Reljic
Martha Wrench

....

Head of Creative Engagement
Romana Flello

Learning Producer
Imogen Fletcher

Participation Producer
Stella Taljaard

Projects Producer
Ella Kennedy

....

Finance Director
Karen Weston

Finance Manager
Daniela Baiocco

....

Fundraising Director
Catherine Walker

Deputy Fundraising Director
Ilaria Pizzichemi

Fundraising Officer
Kirsty Dunn

....

Head of Operations & Front of House
Simon Davis

Catering Manager
Angeliki Apostola

Senior Events Sales Manager
Rebecca Farrow

Front of House & Operations Manager
Laura Barnes

Office & HR Coordinator
Annika Weber

Office & HR Coordinator (Maternity Cover)
Madison Leach

Security Officer
Nagah Elshohady

Duty Managers
Bronya Doyle
Maria Koutsou
Jamie Maier
Willa Main
Moya Matthews
Anna-May Wood

Catering Assistants
Sophie Apthorp
Joe Barber
Saoirse Byrne
Izzy Ajani
Chiara Frídlová
Flo Granger
Martha Haidari
Kate Ivanova
James Lloyd
William Lockey
Willa Main

Orla O'Shea
Amalia Paschalidi
Lois Pearson
Elisa Pedraza
Kerri Purcell
Sandip Valgi

Front of House Assistants
Faizan Ahmed
Amaliyah Allison
Joe Barber
Roo Browning
Izzy Ajani
Saoirse Byrne
Amelie Davies
Martha George
Flo Granger
Martha Haidari
Amal Khalidi
Jaypal Kantilal
Os Leanse
Kirsty Liddell
Anna Lines
Willa Main
Vincenzo Monachello
Temi Majekodunmi
Donia Meftah
Lois Pearson
Ramina Radmard
Rawdat Quadri
Jacqueline Reljic
Rahima Saifuddin
Sandip Valgi
Romario Williams
Martha Wrench
Amy Wright
Amina Zebiri
Yazan Al Nassar
Sala Ogboli

Cleaning Manager
Ragne Kaldoja

Author's Thanks

Philip Norman, Jessica Norman, Hannah Hauer-King, Matthew Waksman, Donald Howarth, Maitreyabandhu, Jnanavaca, Ben Assefa-Folivi, Dylan Aiello, Rebecca Crookshank, Rebecca Latham, Mirain Jones, Jack Holden, James Cooney, Ria Zmitrowicz, Josh Finan, Dickie Beau, Samuel Barnett, Laurie Kynaston, Joel Harper-Jackson, Pearl Mackie, Leo Wan, Nick Fiveash, Shawab Iqbal all the cast, creatives and crew, as well as the entire team at the Kiln Theatre.

Indhu Rubasingham – for her trust, and for inspiring me to think big.

Amit Sharma – for his belief in the play, and for making it happen.

Rikki Beadle-Blair – for everything, always.

For Andrew

With love

Please Please Me

The play takes place during the years between 1957 and 1967, then somewhere outside of time and space. It can be performed with as little as five actors or many more.

Brian Epstein

Soft-spoken with a gentle inner steeliness. Hails from a close middle-class Jewish family. Founder of North End Music Store. Manager of The Beatles and several others. A gentleman, aching from a repressed unexpressed youth.

John Lennon

Lucid, expressive and harsh. Working-class presenting, former art student from Liverpool. Singer, songwriter and musician. Self-proclaimed 'leader' of The Beatles. Poetic, impulsive, mercurial, magnetic.

Cynthia Powell

John Lennon's first serious girlfriend. A diligent art student and aspiring teacher. From 'over the water' on the 'posh' Wirral peninsula. Knows her mind ahead of the times. Faithful to John, despite all the odds.

> *Also plays **Aunt Mimi**, John Lennon's formidable aunt, and **Cilla Black**, Brian's treasured 'songbird', intelligent and elegantly earthly.

Peter Brown

Ex-lover, turned business associate and enduring friend of Brian Epstein. Shapes himself in Brian's image, adopting all of his habits. Including the bad ones.

> *Also plays **Mike Collins**, a passionate young Teddy Boy and **Dizz Gillespie**, an ebullient insightful American street-hustler.

Geoffrey Ellis

Close friend and associate of Brian Epstein. An ambitious high-minded law graduate and a highly articulate conservative gay man. Not a fan of The Beatles or their music.

> *Also plays **Harry Epstein**, Brian Epstein's adoring hard-working father, and **Derek Bellis**, a polite Welsh journalist.

'I don't mind people delving deep into me, searching for reasons and secrets because there is nothing too bad there. Even if there were something to be ashamed of, if it were true and it were known and it were published I could not complain. I am extremely fond of the truth.'

Brian Epstein, *A Cellarful of Noise*

Prologue

Cilla Black   You know our Brian. He never raised his voice. Never needed to. He stood just off to the side and somehow made the whole room – whole world – tilt towards him. Some people fill a space. Brian made one. And once you were inside it, you didn't want to leave.

A heavy guitar riff swamps the stage. Shaking apart the congregation. A silhouette of a sexy Elvis type figure donning a guitar. Screams of thousands and thousands of young girls. The sound of joy. The sound of love. The sound of chaos.

Scene One

The resounding rock chords gradually make way for Max Bruch's Violin Concerto No. 1. 1957. **Brian Epstein** *stands alone in the newly created North End Music Store (NEMS). A banner reads 'Grand Opening'.* **Brian** *approaches a gramophone and changes the Bach to 'Hound Dog' by Elvis Presley. He looks at his reflection and attempts to comb his hair up, like a rockabilly, then immediately flattens it back down with a sigh. Instead he straightens his shirt and tie. His father,* **Harry Epstein**, *hurries through carrying a small box of records, looking bemused at the music.*

Harry (*shouting over the music*)   Which noise is this, then?

Brian   Elvis Presley.

Harry   Pelvis what?

Brian (*holding up the record cover*)   Elvis.

Harry   Good, lord. Is it a man or a woman?

Brian *holds up a Little Richard cover and an Everly Brothers cover.*

Brian   It's what's happening, Dad. This is the new NEMS promise. To obtain any gramophone record a customer desires within three short days. Shipped directly to the glorious port of Liverpool.

Harry   Marvellous. I'll fetch the earplugs.

Brian *takes the record off. They notice a tapping on the window. A young rocker,* **Mike Collins***, is looking in.*

Brian (*calls out through the window*)   We open in an hour.

Brian *moves away nervously organising records.*

Harry   Already queuing up? That's the Epstein effect for you.

Brian   One person.

Harry   Every queue –

Brian   – 'starts with one person'.

Harry *goes over to the window.*

Brian   Can you help me with these?

Harry (*peering out*)   I see he has the Pelvis hair.

Brian   Elvis.

Harry   So our shop is going to be filled with these Eddy boys?

Brian   I'll just finish up out the back.

Harry   Aha! Nervous tummy?

Brian   Daddy!

Harry   Better nervous than witless.

Brian *runs out back, exasperated.* **Mike** *taps on the window again.* **Harry** *looks around. No* **Brian***.*

Harry (*shouting*)   Open!

Mike *steps into the store.*

Harry   Welcome to the North End Music Store – forgive me, NEMS – where you are now enjoying the exclusive one-on-one Epstein experience. I, Harry Epstein, will personally guide you through this labyrinth of musical madness.

Beat.

Are we looking for anything in particular?

Mike   Got any Little Richard?

Harry   We have all the Richards. Now, if you care to follow me, he must be . . . (*Looking around lost.*) Which Richard's the little one?

Mike   'Tutti Frutti'? 'Long Tall Sally'?

Harry   I'm a Mendelssohn man myself.

Harry *leafs hopelessly through the records.*

Harry   Little Richard . . . Would that be under L for ludicrous or R for racket?

Mike   That your lad just now? Looks a bit like you.

Harry   Got my brains too. This is all Brian's hobbyhorse. Records, rock 'n' roll and riffraff – it's his little crusade.

Mike   Boss.

Harry   Every hour, a new idea.

Mike   You let him get on with it though.

Harry   He's soft as butter underneath.

Mike   Was he was always like that?

Harry (*chuckles despite himself*)   When Brian was twelve he announced he was off to be a dressmaker. Wrote it down, very formal. 'Dear Mother and Father . . .' Queenie had to sit down.

Mike (*grinning*)   You're joking.

Harry   Fourteen he's talking about London. Sewing lessons. The lot.

Mike   You weren't mad?

Harry   Just a phase. (*Proudly.*) We sent him to National Service instead.

Mike   I did three years.

Harry   Straighten you out?

Mike   Made me who I am.

A nod of approval.

Mike (*offering his hand*)   Mike.

Brian (*entering*)   Daddy?

Harry   Speak of the devil and he shall appear! I shall now leave you in the supremely capable hands of our modern music messiah, Brian Epstein. Pray for your ears.

Mike *offers* **Brian** *his hand.*

Harry (*introducing*)   Brian. Mike.

Brian *shakes* **Mike***'s hand.*

Brian (*to* **Mike**)   Anything in particular we can we interest you in today?

Harry   He's looking for Little Richard.

Harry *exits to the back.* **Brian** *drops* **Mike***'s hand.*

Brian   You cannot be here.

Mike   I can look at records, can't I? I've got dosh.

Brian *pulls out a Little Richard record and thrusts it to* **Mike**.

Brian   That's four shillings.

Mike   I wanna hear it.

Brian *places the record onto the gramophone. 'Tutti Frutti' plays out.* **Mike** *places four shillings on the counter.* **Brian** *takes the record off, returns it to its sleeve and thrusts it back over to* **Mike**. **Mike** *doesn't take it.*

Mike   This how you treat all your customers? Or is this the 'exclusive one-on-one Epstein experience'?

Brian   I'll call the police.

Mike   Don't look so nervous. This *is* what you offer right? Customer satisfaction? I like your work clobber. (*Stepping in closer.*) Suits you. Proper gentle . . . (*closer again*) man.

Harry *enters with a box of records.* **Mike** *instinctively steps away to look at the stock. He pulls out an Everly Brothers record.*

Mike   Do you think they're really brothers or is that just for show?

He hands **Brian** *the record to play it.* **Brian** *obliges. 'Bye Bye Love'.*

Mike (*listening*)   All the bands cover their songs down the Cavern. You should come down there sometime.

Brian   I'm busy building a business.

Mike   What goes on down the Cavern *is* your business.

He sets down a Cavern leaflet for **Brian**.

I'll take it.

Brian *removes the record, scuffing it slightly.*

Brian   I beg your pardon.

He moves to find another.

Harry (*to* **Mike**)   Don't forget we sell record cabinets too. For your growing racket collection. Do you have a wife and kiddies at home, Mike? We can order beds, cots –

Mike   I'm a bachelor me. Through and through.

Brian *clumsily wraps up the purchases.*

Harry   If Pelvis's eye shadow can get them queuing round the block you'll be coupled up before the autumn.

Brian *hands* **Mike** *his goods.* **Harry** *returns to the back.* **Mike** *seizes the moment, planting a kiss on* **Brian**. *Stunned,* **Brian** *hesitates, then abruptly pushes* **Mike** *away.* **Mike** *stumbles back, then instinctively raises his fist.* **Brian** *flinches, but doesn't retreat. Fear, yes – but something else flickers underneath it.* **Mike** *sees it.*

Mike   There it is. (*His gaze drops to* **Brian**'s *crotch.*) Look at you. Excited Daddy's here. (*Checking the door, stepping closer.*) Three strokes. (*His hand brushes over* **Brian**'s *groin.*) Just like always.

Brian *jerks away.*

Mike   How many lads have you had chasing you in here, then?

Brian   None.

Mike   Bet you will though.

Brian   Please. I'm begging you.

Mike   So this is how it feels to have all the power. Beg me some more.

Brian   Please.

Mike   You said you were gunna take us to London. Show me off to your posh drama school mates.

Brian   You know you're not the issue.

Mike   Remember that time we named each star down the dock? You called me your little duckling. Made me promise we'd swim off together.

Brian   You hated that –

Mike   That we'd somehow make something of ourselves. Together.

Brian (*desperate*)   What do you want?

Mike   Tonight. My folks are in Blackpool.

Brian   I'm busy tonight.

Mike   Tomorrow then. Meet me at our hotel. I'll pay this time.

Brian   Mikey, no.

Mike   Why am I saving for that shitty motorbike anyway? I ain't going nowhere.

Brian   I said no.

Mike   So I'm dumped then? A bit of rough you used to like to fuck –

Brian   Shhh.

Mike   – and now you've used me up, you wanna chuck me away like bog roll?

Brian   I'm afraid I'm going to have ask you to leave.

Mike (*hissing*)   Don't tell me what to fucking do!

Brian   Okay! Okay . . .

Mike   Look around at how fucking jammy you are. Building this whole business just to lure in all the good-looking lads with your fancy hi-fi gramophone. At least the other phoneys gave me money. What am I getting, Brian? Besides a drawn and fucking quartered heart?

Brian *get out his wallet.*

Mike   What the fuck are you doing?

Brian   What you're asking of me. You're blackmailing me aren't you?

Mike *thumps* **Brian** *in the face.* **Brian** *screams.*

Mike   You bastard! If I wanted your wallet I'd have fucking taken it.

Brian   Please, Mikey!

Harry (*rushing in*)   Get away from him!

Mike (*to* **Brian**)   I was a proper man before you turned me into this.

Harry   What is wrong with you?!

Mike (*to* **Brian**)   Ruined me so no lass could possibly want me.

Harry   Pardon?

Mike   You heard. Your son's a pervert. He corrupted me. Now . . . I want money.

Mike'*s eyes flicker between* **Harry** *and* **Brian**.

Harry   One hundred?

Mike *shakes his head.*

Harry   One hundred and fifty. Final offer.

Mike (*firmly*)   Three.

Harry *takes out his cheque book.*

Mike   Three fifty.

Harry *sighs and continues.*

Mike   You must really love your precious little pansy.

Harry *holds out the cheque.* **Mike** *doesn't move.* **Harry** *tries to press it into his hand, but* **Mike** *refuses, his gaze fixed on* **Brian**. *A tense beat.* **Harry** *exhales, slipping the cheque into* **Mike**'*s pocket and giving him a long gentle push backwards towards the door.* **Mike** *doesn't resist, his eyes never leaving* **Brian**. *Then, just as they reach the door,* **Mike** *suddenly grabs* **Harry** *forcefully by the lapels, then pulls him into a tight, unexpected hug.* **Harry** *stiffens, caught off guard, his hands hovering uncertainly. After a moment,* **Mike** *lets go. Then, without hesitation, he spits in* **Brian**'*s face.* **Mike** *almost goes to wipe it off himself, but pulls back, and rushes out.* **Brian** *and* **Harry** *remaining frozen, unable to meet each other's eyes. The silence hang heavy between them. Beat. Then* **Harry** *exhales and quietly returns to work as if nothing has happened.*

Brain Epstein   I'll pay you back. Every penny.

Harry *ignores him.* **Brian** *begins to work too. The silence grows more and more excruciating.* **Brian** *jerks to a halt, letting out a small, uncontrollable, animal-like whimper, which* **Harry** *completely ignores.*

Brain Epstein   I know . . . I'm not the son you wanted . . .

Harry   We don't always get what we want.

Brian *notices* **Harry**'s *hands shaking with barely suppressed rage.*

Brian   What if he comes back? Father?

Beat.

I think he'll come back, Daddy.

Harry *stops. Then picks up the phone.*

Brian   Who are you calling? (**Brian** *puts his hand over the phone.*) We can't call the police!

Harry   Do you want this sorted or not?

Brian   What if they believe him?

Harry   You're an Epstein. You have no criminal record. They'll look at him and they'll look at you and they'll know he's telling lies.

Brian   We can't just ruin his whole life.

Harry   You'd rather him ruin yours?

Harry *begins to dial again.*

Brian   I have a record.

Beat.

I was . . . arrested. I'm due in court in two months.

Harry   What on earth did you do?

Brian   I didn't do anything. I just . . . wanted to.

Harry   Think about what you're admitting to.

Brian   They always make the first move. I'm just there. Powerless. I try to resist. But I think it's something in me. Something uncontrollable. Although I know I must.

Harry   What do you want from me?

Brian   Please, Mother can't know.

Harry   You think I'd do that to her? Destroy the only pure thing left in my life? I would sooner die than let your mother hear the truth of what you are. You really want me to say it out loud? That you've brought shame into this shop like a plague? You've taken our name – this family's history – and dragged it through the gutter. Look at me. How am I meant to walk into shul with all those eyes burning through me – whispering, judging? You are my boy. My beautiful boy. I kissed your forehead every night and thanked the almighty for you. Now? Now I look at you . . . And I have no words left.

He exits, leaving **Brian** *alone and broken. After a moment, he notices the Cavern leaflet. Picks it up.*

Scene Two

We are led through time and space by 'Kilimanjaro' by Quartette Trés Bien. 1961.

Brian   Sweat and cologne. The thick hot stench hits me like a fist. What on earth am I doing here? This was supposed to be just another ordinary lunch break. Yet somehow here I am. Hovering nervously on the threshold. Drawn by an irresistible urge to step inside. Turn back. But my body betrays me with every step down into the underworld. Shadowy bodies all facing away. Everyone looking in one direction. Panic rises. I don't belong here. I'm nothing like them, turn back. And then I hear what everyone else hears.

I'm pulled stumbling forward. And I see what everyone else sees.

The piano is replaced with the up-tempo guitar of 'My Bonnie' covered by The Beatles. The Cavern Club bursts into life.

Brian   Four towering man boys. Poured into jet-black well-worn leather. Larking. Swaggering. Smoking. Swearing. Shamelessly joyously sweaty. Their quiffs flicking beads of wet testosterone over and into the crowd. Their 'performance' is a chaotic display of appalling arrogance and utterly irresistible charm. Gosh. That sound. It's rock and roll but so much more. The bizarre screaming. Such tantalising wailing. When they start playing their music the entire disordered world slips and slides on its axis, to the pulse of their magnificent beat. Beat music. As John cocks his head back to snigger with his slight sexy sneer, every girl in the room faints on her feet. I'm lost dreaming up LP covers. Dance hall posters. Struck by an unstoppable vision and unquestionable faith in their ability to change the world. Conjuring an existence in which I'm the one to help them thrive. When booming over the speaker system, like the voice of God himself, I hear –

John Lennon   Mr Epstein from NEMS. Welcome to the Cavern.

The music stumbles to a halt. Cheers and whistles ripple through the crowd. **John** *leans into the microphone, peering through the lights.*

John   Where's he hiding then? Our mysterious shopkeeper.

Brian *freezes.* **John** *locks eyes with him.*

John   Oh, I see. You lost, love?

Laughter from the room. **Brian** *doesn't rise to it.*

Brian   I came to hear the music.

John   Did you now?

Beat. **John** *studies him.*

John   And?

Brian   I'm still listening.

John   Careful, Mr Epstein. Stay too long down here, you might start enjoying yourself.

Brian   I rather think I already am.

They hold each other's gaze a moment longer than necessary. **John** *breaks, turning back to the band.*

John   Right then, lads. Let's give the man something worth selling.

We are now inside the NEMS office. **Brian** *is talking to his employee and friend,* **Peter Brown**.

Peter   I'm surprised it's your kind of sound.

Brian   Peter, The Beatles are everybody's sound.

Peter   I have a girlfriend who –

Brian   Girlfriend?

Peter   Girl-*friend* – who scurries directly to the Cavern every lunchtime, without exception, just to catch a brief glimpse of their sweaty foreheads. (*Putting on* **Brian**'s *tie.*) Once she was told there wasn't enough room, so she ran round the back and climbed through the window of the bogs. No matter how hard she squeezed she just couldn't wriggle her hips through the gap. It was two hours before someone found her. Still buzzing to have overheard even the faintest echoes of John and Paul's banter through the swinging doors of the smelly stalls.

Brian   Marvellous! Aren't they utterly sensational?

Peter   Sensational.

He finishes the tie with a flourish.

Peter   How did you introduce yourself?

Brian   I went right up to John – butterflies flooding my stomach – and said, 'I'd like to be your manager.'

Peter   You're sweating!

Brian   I'm hypnotised. Until that moment, I'd never even thought about being a manager of a band!

Peter   You're not yet.

Brian (*pacing, excitedly*)   Where is he with those signatures?

Peter   Is a formal agreement a good idea this early doors?

Brian (*ignoring* **Peter**)   It's but a half-hour drive from either Allerton or Mendips.

Peter   Who lives in Mendips?

Brian   John. They still have the servants' bell outside the door.

Peter   I thought these boys were proper Scousers.

Brian   They are. That's their beauty. Basically. Except John who's from surprisingly respectable stock. And his Aunt Mimi is the bones and gristle.

Peter   Bit of a battle axe?

Brian   Don't get nervous now. She'll be hopping off the bus outside any moment.

Peter (*handing* **Brian** *his case*)   Didn't fancy chauffeuring her in that snazzy car of yours then?

Brian   She refused. She's a tough nut to crack, but crack her we must.

Peter   Mimi's the mission. John is the goal?

Brian (*uncomfortable*)   John thinks of himself as the unofficial leader of the band. Mimi has John's ear. Get Mimi on side then we are one step closer to having The Beatles.

Peter   Do you really need these lads when you're so busy here at NEMS, mesmerising the youth of Liverpool into shelling out for whatever record you think they need?

Brian   I need a new challenge. You need space to spread your wings. Find your own protégé to train up. That'd keep your hands full for a while.

Peter   There's nothing wrong with being made up with what you have. Savouring life's simple pleasures and just enjoying the view for a little while.

Brian   A provincial view.

Peter   Liverpool is not a province. You've barely got this store to where you imagined it and you're off chasing another pipe dream. I adore you, Brian, but Christ alive, do you ever rest?

Brian   There's a big world out there. The Beatles could be a golden ticket for all at NEMS to grab hold of.

Peter   Won't Daddy be fuming?

Brian   He needn't know anything for now.

Peter   He'll grill me.

Brian   Don't tell tales until we're ready.

Peter   Your lawyer is very loyal to your father. He'll spill about the contracts.

Brian   I took them to Geoffrey instead.

Peter *rolls his eyes.*

Brian   Geoffrey's going to be a terrific lawyer when he's qualified and he's a very loyal friend. (*Checking the time.*) If slightly behind schedule.

Peter   He's a pretentious, self-centred bore, whose entire identity is wrapped up in having studied at Oxford and feeling massively superior to scallies like us.

Brian   What has dear Geoffrey ever done to you?

Peter   Geoffrey will blab to your father just to be certain you won't outdo him.

Brian   Never mind Geoffrey. What Daddy wants more than anything is to be proud of his son. By the time anyone is silly enough to divulge my plans, the boys will already be bigger than Elvis.

Peter   Elvis? You've lost your mind.

Brian   I've never been more certain about anything in my life.

Peter   I hope you've purified your intentions with these boys, Mr Epstein.

Brian   Our partnership is strictly professional.

Peter   So was ours. Until it wasn't.

Brian   And now it is again.

He looks uncomfortable.

You were the one who came after me, remember?

Peter   As I recall, I was poached – after you witnessed my exceptional sales technique.

Brian   I recognise talent when I see it.

Peter   Compensated, I might add, with a pay cut.

Brian   In return I've given you a more stimulating livelihood. Not to mention an honest friendship. Aren't you satisfied with what we're building?

Peter   That's exactly why I'd rather drag your suspiciously well-coiffed head back below the parapet – where it's safe. (**Brian** *sighs*.) If your Beatles find out you sleep with men, what then?

Brian   Then I'll stop.

Peter   Just like that?

Brian   What's the point?

Peter   Brian, being in the spotlight –

Brian   Means being *immaculate* forever. I understand. I comply. And in return, we bask in success. So tell me, do you wish to come on this adventure or not?

Peter   With you?

Brian   Me and the boys.

Peter   Boys? Or boy?

A knock at the door.

Brian   Not a word more.

Peter   Just smiles and compliments.

Brian (*looking outside*)   Geoffrey was meant to be here . . .

Peter   God, why am I more nervous about Mimi than I was when the lads came here?

Brian   Just leave her to me. Now fetch her in please.

Peter *exits briefly.* **Brian** *takes a moment to perfect his tie.* **Peter** *hastily returns, followed by* **Aunt Mimi**.

Brian   Good afternoon, Mrs Smith. What an honour to have you grace our humble store.

Aunt Mimi   Didn't get such a greeting last time I was here.

Brian   Then it can't have been me managing the floor.

Peter   Maybe you've confused us with another establishment.

Aunt Mimi   I don't get confused. When my George purchased us the house on Menlove Avenue –

Brian   Mendips? Outstanding property.

Aunt Mimi   – I came in here all full of meself. Cash in hand, no credit, ready to furnish the entire place. Five minutes later I'm back on the street, with a lump in my throat, heading for a more welcoming establishment.

Brian   You must have visited the store before 1957. My daddy did a terrific job building this company, but it was always clear to me that the way the furniture was presented and the general ambience was out of step with the people.

Peter   Brian changed all that. The choice of product, the presentation, the entire customer experience.

Brian   Under my leadership, each display became a work of art, that everyone could enjoy.

Aunt Mimi   Boys are a bit different than settees, I think you'll find. What makes you think you can buy and sell them? Why would you want to risk the security of an established family business?

Brian   There's a different sort of security in certain kinds of risk.

Peter   You won't meet a man as extraordinary as Brian, Miss Smith.

Brian   Peter, there's no need to –

Aunt Mimi   No, please. Pontificate.

Peter   Brian believes in himself. And he's always looking for ways to test that belief. He won't ever allow himself to lose.

Aunt Mimi   I was married to a gambling man and I wasn't afraid to kick him out of the house he paid for.

Brian (*smiling graciously*)   Peter has been my personal assistant for almost three years now. (**Peter** *throws* **Brian** *a look – he's no assistant.*) I've always adored investing in gifted individuals. May I have a moment to outline my business plan?

Aunt Mimi   Oh, am I interrupting?

Brian   I know what you're thinking. I'm no big time music executive.

Peter   Yet . . .

Brian   But through building this business by hand, I have made connections in the music industry that can immediately secure the boys better engagements. Opportunities to record their music professionally. Even sign with a major record label.

Aunt Mimi   Just like that?

Brian   With the power of North End Music Store behind them, I can ensure their first record reaches number one. I know what young people want and I think I know how to give it to them. When the world encounters our boys, I'm certain they will fall in love, just as we have.

Aunt Mimi   In love?

Brian   In love.

Beat.

Aunt Mimi   What does your wife think of this new venture?

Brian   No wife, Mrs Smith. (*Seeing* **Mimi***'s reaction, smoothly.*) But I am optimistically courting that delightful secretary you met downstairs.

Mimi *frowns, suspicious.* **Peter** *throws* **Brian** *a knowing look.*

Aunt Mimi   And your family?

Brian   They do what families do – they support me.

Aunt Mimi   I'm family. And even I haven't bothered to see him play.

Brian   Hence my strategy to overcome The Beatles' first major obstacle.

Aunt Mimi   Me?

Brian   Everyone at the Cavern loves The Beatles. But how do we make everyone outside the Cavern feel the same? With a fresh presentation. All the leather, the smoking, crudeness might appeal to the provincial young, but you and I both know that any right-minded parent would never let their child bring one of their records home. Now picture John and the boys in suits. Trendy, but smart. Tidier haircuts . . . All their charm, wit, appeal, presented in a way that is just a pinch of naughty but, crucially, family friendly. Something a mother could be proud of. You are our litmus test. Our objective rational eyes and ears. We need you on the team, Mrs Smith.

Aunt Mimi (*laughing knowingly*)   John won't change. Certainly not for me.

Brian   John wants success. Given a choice between mucking around in a basement, playing nine-hour sets, or earning one hundred pounds an hour at the Liverpool Odeon, what do you think he'll choose?

Aunt Mimi   So it's all about the money?

Brian   I shan't take any profit until there's enough to pay them all and some left over. In fact, I'll be paying them out of my own pocket to begin with. Money earned from NEMS.

Aunt Mimi   Are you mad?

Brian   You might say I'm mad about the boys. The Beatles are really something special. And they're going to be stars. All of them.

Aunt Mimi   And you? Are you . . . special?

Brian   Better. I'm deeply committed.

Aunt Mimi   And if you're deeply wrong?

Brian   Then The Beatles will have travelled the globe. Amassed enough earnings to buy a house. Saved a little more for the future. And they return home to their families with stories for their grandchildren.

Aunt Mimi   Not John. John's never going to make a little nest egg and settle down in the suburbs. If he goes with you, he'll become a travelling man. Just like his good-for-nothing father. *You* might settle down when you've got what you want out of him, but I know you're taking my boy away from me for good.

Brian   I promise you, I'll always take care of your John.

Aunt Mimi   Are you sure you know what you're letting yourself in for?

Beat. **Brian** *considers.*

Aunt Mimi   You can put him in a shirt and tie, but he'll always be himself.

Brian   That's precisely what –

Aunt Mimi   John has relished being the wild teenager. According to the parents of the few friends he has left, he's the wildest. At one point it was an ongoing miracle that he swerved prison. I was at my wits' end when I gave in and let him go to art school. And of course it worked. Finally there was a place where he could channel all of that unstoppable energy.

Brian *sits, listening attentively.*

Aunt Mimi   Because the inconvenient truth that I have to admit, Mr Epstein, is that he's not my son. He's Julia's. And he's got Julia's spirit. I bought him books, Julia bought him a banjo. I gave him discipline, he used it to learn the guitar. I fed him nutritious food, she fed him his first Eddie Cochran record. It's always been a battle between the books and the banjo. Even with all the fear, grief and anxiety that boy has had to suffer – or maybe because of it – the banjo has won. (*Looking at her watch.*) And my bus leaves in five minutes.

Brian   When's the next one? (*Stalling.*) You mustn't leave without Peter acquainting you with our fresh new collection. (*Ushering* **Peter**.) Direct from artisans in East Tennessee.

Peter   The rocking chairs are my favourite. Come let's get you swinging in one.

As **Mimi** *begins to steam,* **Geoffrey Ellis** *burst into the office, with a self-assured flounce.*

Geoffrey   I know, I know! You might have warned me they behave like Maria bloody Callas. Why do you want four divas? If you'd followed my suggestion and pursued classical, you'd only have one.

Brian   Geoffrey, may I introduce you to –

Peter (*to* **Geoffrey**)   What took you so long?

Geoffrey   They were in the middle of playing one of their little ditties. It did sound interesting, I have to say, I'm starting to understand why you think these beatniks might be any good.

They're no Rachmaninoff, but –

Brian *impatiently holds out his hand so that* **Geoffrey** *passes him the contract, still donning a smug impression.* **Brian** *immediately scans through the document.*

Geoffrey   They didn't even look at it in the end.

Peter (*to* **Aunt Mimi**)   Mrs Smith. This is a chance for John to really make something out of all your hard work.

The penny drops for **Geoffrey** *as he realises who* **Aunt Mimi** *is.*

Geoffrey (*to* **Aunt Mimi**, *forced*)   Brian believes in himself. And he's always looking for –

Peter *elbows him.* **Brian** *holds the contract out to* **Mimi**, *who receives it cautiously.*

Brian   This agreement is between myself . . . George Harrison, Pete Best, James Paul McCartney and John Winston Lennon, hereinafter called The Beatles . . .

Aunt Mimi (*reading*)   They've already signed.

Brian   But I haven't. I don't want to trap them into something that isn't right. Not until I've proven myself.

Geoffrey   Er, Brian . . . (*Discreetly.*) Then there's nothing stopping them using you and walking away.

Brian   If they want to. So I'd better do my job. (*To* **Aunt Mimi**.) This is how much I believe in him.

Aunt Mimi *hands the contract back. Turns to leave. For a moment,* **Brian** *looks crestfallen.*

Aunt Mimi   Mohair. (*Approaching the door.*) For the suits.

She leaves.

Geoffrey   I hope you know what you're doing, Brian.

Brian (*shelving the contract*)   We stand on the brink of introducing the Mersey sound to the masses. Heralding a revolution that everyone can be part of.

Peter   Everyone?

Brian   Everyone. Is there anything more important than this?

Scene Three

Brian Epstein *closes his eyes, as if making a wish, his expression softening. We hear the lush strings of 'All My Loving' (the George Martin Orchestra version), blossoming in his mind. She slips into his tailored coat, smoothing it down with nervous precision. 1962.* **Brian** *descends into the Cavern Club, where he's greeted by the buoyant cloakroom attendant,* **Cilla Black**.

Cilla   Take your coat, love?

Brian   No need, thank you.

Cilla   You'll sweat yourself dead wearing all that in there!

Brian   I shan't stay long.

Cilla   Giz it here! Pinky swear I won't nick owt. I'll even do you a wee discount if you're skint.

She offers a wink. **Brian** *smiles. Hands over his jacket.*

Cilla   You a bizzy?

Brian   A what?

Cilla   Old Bill. Peelers. Police!

Brian   Er, no, I –

Cilla   Mmm. (*Peaking at the label of* **Brian***'s coat.*) Savile Row? Very nice. (*Handing* **Brian** *his ticket.*) Mr Epstein, I presume?

Brian   Do I stand out that much?

Cilla   For all the right reasons. Distinguished.

Brian (*extending his hand*)   Brian.

Cilla (*takes his hand, leaning in conspiratorially*)   I advise you to use a codename or all the Lennon wannabes will eat you alive.

Brian *shifts uncomfortably.*

Cilla   Don't worry, pet. All your secrets are safe with me. (*Pointing.*) See that spot over there? It might not look owt, but that there is the finest view in the house. Sound is dead good an' all. And the best bit; the light above is knackered. Leaving you, lovely la-di-dah Brian, totally incognito. I sneak out there myself when I'm on shift. Wanna take a bevvie with ya? What's your tipple? Whiskey? Rum? Brandy? We have all the spirits down 'ere.

Brian   Regrettably, I must resist. I'm here on business.

Cilla   Ah yes. The business of show. Not long now before those record companies wake up and see what us Scousers can do. How many acts you signed now?

Brian   A handful.

Cilla   None like The Beatles though. You must be made up.

Brian   It's all just part of the plan.

Cilla   You'll be down in London soon, I reckon. That's what our John says.

Brian   You know John?

Cilla   I know everyone and everyone knows me. Cloakroom girl, superstar.

She cringes worrying she's overstepped. This inadvertently warms **Brian** *to her.*

Brian   I'm actually here to see a new act.

Cilla   Oh yeah? Heard good things?

Brian   Honestly?

Cilla   Always.

Brian   I've heard very little. The Beatles – well, *John's* recommended her. Probably some dolly bird he desperately wants to impress. (*Adopting a gossipy whisper.*) He's offering up a convincing turn that they're just 'friends'. Even got the mighty Aunt Mimi to bat for her.

Cilla   Ooh! She must be dead good then. It's much harder for girls at the Cavern.

Brian   Oh?

Cilla   Cutting through the screams of swarming teenage girls who only wanna trample her and grab the mic themselves? She must have balls of steel and a solid pair of lungs if she can impress these hyenas.

Brian *ponders for a moment.*

Cilla   Would you ever sign a girl? Honestly?

Brian   Honestly? I suppose I've never quite got women. I think I know how to sell *to* them. But to market them? To build a partnership? It's something quite different.

Cilla   What's wrong with something different?

Beat. **Cilla** *smiles.*

Cilla   Live and let live I say.

Brian *smiles with uncertain relief. Behind him,* **Mike Collins** *arrives.*

Mike (*to* **Cilla**)   Alright, Scarlet O'Scouser.

Cilla   Alright, Mikey! When we getting married again?

Mike   When you gunna ask me?

Mike *hands* **Cilla** *his jacket.*

Cilla   Isn't it a leap year next year?

Mike   What's that got to do with a proposal or the price of tea?

Cilla   Don't ya know? Every fourth year the girls can do the asking.

Mike   I'll be sat up on my hind legs waiting.

Cilla   There's a good boy. (*Handing* **Mike** *his ticket.*) Fetch.

As **Mike** *turns he comes face to face with* **Brian**.

Cilla (*to* **Mike**)   Now you run along and play with the other puppies in the playground.

Brian *moves, allowing* **Mike** *to get through.*

Cilla (*to* **Brian**)   Mikey's a character.

Brian   Indeed.

Cilla   Done time for it too, poor thing. But I quite like that in a man. Character.

Brian *offers his ticket back.* **Cilla** *looks at it puzzled.*

Brian (*asserting*)   May I have my coat?

Cilla   Y'what? You can't go now!

Brian   Why not?

Cilla   Your new starlet will be busting a gut to meet you.

Brian   She needn't know I came.

John (*off stage, amplified*)   Alright, you charming rabble.

Cilla *steps out of the booth. The intro vamp to 'Fever' by Peggy Lee begins.*

Cilla   John'll only drag you back another time. (*Haphazardly strapping on different shoes.*) Stay. It won't take long.

John (*off stage, amplified*)   It's time to welcome to the stage Merseyside's own, Pricilla Black!

Cilla (*correcting*)   White!

An unsteady follow spot is directed towards **Cilla**.

Brian   You?!

Cilla   I'd kiss ya for luck, but I'm wearing lippy!

Brian *is flabbergasted.* **Cilla** *hastily slaps powder on her cheeks.*

Cilla   Lovely to meet you, Bri. (*Pulling* **Brian** *in for a hug.*) Stay.

Cilla *flashes* **Brian** *her trademark cheeky grin before dashing onto the stage.* **Brian** *looks on, secretly impressed, as 'Fever' takes off.*

Scene Four

The sexy rocker silhouette appears again, but this time it turns, revealing a slightly protruding pregnant belly. 1962. In the NEMS office, **Geoffrey Ellis** *has burst in on* **Brian Epstein** *– coat still on, a poster clutched in his hand – clearly not intending to stay.*

Geoffrey   You've reordered the billing.

Brian   I'm clarifying it.

Geoffrey   You've put Lennon first.

Brian (*without looking up*)   He is first.

Geoffrey   That's not what the contract says.

Brian   Then change the contract.

Beat.

What? It's business.

Geoffrey   You're rewriting the band around one man.

Brian   I'm protecting its centre of gravity.

Geoffrey   You're confusing gravity with attachment.

Brian   Must you always mistrust passion?

Geoffrey   Unexamined passion.

Brian   As much as I respect your legal opinion, Geoffrey, you wouldn't recognise genius if it insulted you.

Geoffrey   Trust me – he does, on a weekly basis.

Brian   John is difficult because he is *alive*.

Geoffrey   Like a grenade.

Brian   He's irreplaceable.

Geoffrey   No one is.

Brian   You don't hear what I hear.

Geoffrey   I hear a man rearranging his life. For what? Some vague hope he might glance your way a little longer? Or treat a contract like a love letter?

Brian   Everything I do is for the band.

Geoffrey   You spend more time 'managing' John than the others combined.

Brian   We're friends.

Geoffrey   How neat.

Brian   Now now. You're tittering on insulting.

Geoffrey   You've given him discretion no one else gets.

Brian   Because he'll push back.

Geoffrey   You speak about him like he's a force of nature, and you've decided you're the only man who can contain him.

Brian   Someone has to.

Geoffrey   Because you enjoy it?

Brian   Because if he fractures, everything fractures.

Geoffrey   Or because if he leaves, you do.

A knock at the door. **Brian** *smooths his tie, reflexive.*

Brian   That'll be John.

Geoffrey   I've done all I can for you and NEMS.

Brian   Geoffrey –

Geoffrey   I'm sailing for New York next month. Try not to let the empire collapse before I get there.

He heads for the door.

Remember who's managing who. Devotion makes a fine servant, Brian, but it can be dangerous master.

He exits. A softer knock.

Brian   Come in.

Cynthia Powell *enters.*

Brian   Cynthia . . .

Cynthia   I won't keep you.

Brian   No, come in.

He gestures to the chair. She remains standing.

Cynthia   I thought it better you heard it from me.

Brian   He hasn't been arrested again, has he?

Cynthia   Not yet.

A small breath.

Cynthia   Fifteen weeks.

Brian   I'm sorry?

Cynthia   Fifteen weeks. (*Touching her stomach.*) Give or take.

Beat.

Brian   And John knows this?

Cynthia   He keeps promising he's gunna tell you. I don't know what he's so afraid of.

Beat.

Brian?

Brian   Have you thought about what you want to do?

Cynthia   What I want to . . .?

Brian   You're doing so well with your teaching training.

Cynthia *looks away.*

Brian   Though John can be a terrific distraction.

Cynthia   I failed my final exam.

Brian   Perhaps that's a good thing. You're quite the talented artist you know. We'll instruct young Mr Lennon to give you room enough to get back to what you really love.

Cynthia   It might be too much with a baby.

Brian   We can help with that.

Cynthia   Oh, Brian, really?

Brian   Of course. There are certain people who deal with this sort of thing all the time.

Cynthia   Oh I see. Thank you. But the thing is . . . John says he wants us to keep –

Brian   I'll speak to John.

Cynthia's *lip starts to quiver.*

Brian   It's okay.

Brian *delicately perfects a small smudge just above* **Cynthia**'s *lip.*

Brian   It is somewhat overwhelming. All of this just as we're finally about to secure a recording contract.

Cynthia   I thought Decca said no?

Brian   We never wanted Decca.

Cynthia   Epsilon, Capitol Records, EMI . . . You've been promising a deal for months.

Brian   We have a new lead at EMI. He likes them, Cynthia. I think he's a believer. When he inevitably agrees to record 'Love Me Do' it'll quickly become number one. You've seen how crowds respond to the boys. It's only a matter of time.

Cynthia   How can you be sure?

Brian   You don't believe in him?

Cynthia   It's not happening, Brian. Not right now at least.

Brian *pulls out a hanky and offers it to her.*

Cynthia   John and I have been talking and we think this is as good a time as any for us to move forward. You can't expect him to throw away his first proper chance for a real family. And for what? A bucket of air?

Brian   Months of calls and meetings. Dinners spent chasing every lead, flattering A&R men, sending demos, rehearsing pitches until I'm hoarse. Riding the London Express so often they'll name a bench after me at Lime Street – all to persuade someone to take a chance on a Liverpool band no one outside Liverpool or Hamburg has ever heard of.

Cynthia   We're really very grateful.

Brian   Wining and dining label execs just to let the boys play their own songs. Giving Pete the awkward chop and easing Ringo into their so-called all-star line-up. Standing at John's side while his voice cracks with nerves.

Cynthia   I'd come if you'd let me.

Brian   Every step has been a balancing act. I've leveraged every contact, every scrap of good will I've earned – disobeying Daddy's wishes and disregarding my own – all to keep the boys happy and get them what they deserve.

Cynthia   And I'm in the way?

Brian   Of course not, my love.

He takes the hanky, dabs her eyes and then gets her to delicately blow her nose into it.

Cynthia   Oh I know I'm in the way. And I know this baby's in the way. I don't know what's happening, Brian. I was gunna be Georgia O'Keeffe. I was the one who was going to get out of Liverpool and make something marvellous of myself. The furthest thing from some poor cow with six kids pulling at her frock and a no-good husband who's resident at the betting office and the local. Then one tap on my shoulder in calligraphy class and a sarky flirty comment from a gorgeous boy with a quiff, and I'm lending him my pencils and hanging on his every word. I know that's not the kind of woman John wants. That he wants – needs – to conquer the world. But I also know that impulsively – irrationally – he wants this baby. And somehow out of nowhere, so do I. Wouldn't you, Brian? Special men make special babies. And John is . . . (*Sighs.*) When he sings me songs of wild love he's written while I'm asleep . . . How am I gunna deny that wildness? How am I gunna tell a genius to come home early to sit in front of the telly, bouncing a crying baby on his knee? But how can I refuse to have that baby?

Beat.

Brian   Well, there's only one thing a proper gentleman must do. John must propose.

Cynthia   But you're creating an image of John as this fun-loving sweet cheeky chappie who –

Brian   Does the right thing. John needs to marry you.

Cynthia   You serious? You said Beatles can't have wives.

Brian   They can't have an illegitimate child either. You're getting married. I'll give you away myself.

Cynthia   You might have to discuss that my father.

Brian   I'll arrange everything. You won't have to worry about a thing.

Cynthia   And if John doesn't want to marry me?

Brian   He will. He does. Other people don't know John. But you and I do. The ceremony will have to be very private, of course. For your safety and the baby's. As you know, the devotion of these Liverpool girls can be quite ferocious.

Cynthia   So can mine.

Brian   Close your eyes.

Cynthia   Brian . . .

Brian   Just do as I say, Cyn, darling.

Cynthia *closes her eyes.* **Brian** *rummages around slightly then hands her a set of keys.* **Cynthia** *opens her eyes and looks at* **Brian** *unsure.*

Cynthia   Keys?

Brian   To my flat.

Cynthia   But you kip with your family?

Brian   I just bought the flat as an investment. And for . . . socialising.

Cynthia   Oh.

Brian   I want you and John to live in it.

Cynthia   With you?

Brian   No, but I'll be there whenever you need me. It's no use you staying with Mimi. You need to be together with the baby in your own space. Start your family the proper way.

Cynthia   Brian, it's too much.

Brian   You don't have to move in straight away.

Cynthia   We're perfectly fine living with Mimi.

Brian   She calls you a gangster's moll.

Cynthia   I'm growing on her.

Brian   John told me she threw a mirror at you! I won't charge you a penny. I can even arrange a living expense.

Cynthia (*laughing, but not necessarily joyfully*)   Why do I get the feeling you're going to turn up at our honeymoon?

Brian   Only if there's work to be done. No need for concern. John loves you. And I love you too. You'll always be in his music. You'll always be in his life. John is yours.

The intrusive harmonica of 'Love Me Do' by The Beatles. As the lyrics begin, a new- born cries, growing louder and louder, until it's drowned out by the music transitioning through 'Ask Me Why' and into 'From Me to You' by The Beatles. The sound of applause and cheering slowly increasing throughout.

Scene Five

1963. A hotel bedroom in Torremolinos. Two single beds pushed together. One side of the room is a total mess – clothes strewn, left-over drinks glasses, cigarette ash, acoustic guitar; on the other everything is folded immaculately. **John Lennon** *tumbles into the room, bottle of champagne in hand, followed excitedly by* **Brian Epstein**.

John   Back to the shag pad. Men only. Boys only. *Ombres* only!

Brian (*locking the door*)   Shhh! The hotel staff might not know who you are, but this place is full of tourists.

John   Tourist scum. *Viva* España!

Brian   There were definitely more than a few nudges on our plane.

John   Not as many as there will be. (*Popping the cork.*) *Salut!*

John *pours out the champagne into two glasses. Gives one to* **Brian**.

John (*toasting*)   To finally being *numbero uno* in the hit parade!

Brian (*clinking glasses*)   To *Please Please Me* – a remarkable debut album. And for making me the proudest manager in the world.

John   Can you believe we're going to play the Royal Albert Hall?

Brian   I always said, once we had a number one, everything would follow.

John   Better sharpen up my patter. Don't wanna scare off the poshos.

Brian   Being yourself has got you this far.

John   Reckon our next record will hit number one too?

Brian   And the next. Then the one after that.

John   Jesus. We don't want to be working that long.

Brian   Then we better think of other financial avenues. America for starters.

John   You're off your fucking head!

Brian   They're going to love you.

John (*speaking posh*)   Then I really will have to work on my posho voice.

Brian (*attempting* **John**'s *accent*)   They'll 'ave wot we give 'em.

John   Are you sure you're a Scouser? Or did aliens drop you on the banks of the Mersey?

Brian (*enjoying it*)   Shush now!

John   No teenage girls are staying at the Hotel Avenida Palace. If you can't be yourself here, why did you bring us?

Brian   Why did you agree to come with me? You could be tanning it up with the boys in Tenerife, wild as you like.

John   Leaving you on your bill? All I need's for you to embrace your inner flamenco, before I get swamped with regret.

Brian (*checking the door*)   Even in Spain there are rules.

John   But it's not the same. I've been doing my research. (*Indicates the area.*) Bohemia!

Brian *sips his champagne.* **John** *immediately tops him up.*

Brian   Even in 'bohemia' certain behaviours are acceptable and others aren't. There's a different code in bars such as where we resided this afternoon, for example, than if we were walking down by the beach. Or had met at the bathhouse.

John   Fucking 'ell. It's a whole other world.

Brian   There are important signals. Unspoken boundaries. An understanding between men of the same disposition, that turns the cogs on our clandestine machinations.

John   My my. We have a little McCartney amongst us!

Brian   Don't be absurd.

John   Paulo McCartney. Writer of lyrics. Words. Romantico words. Very specialey. (**Brian** *blushes.*) Have you ever pulled in a public bog? Isn't that what your lot do back in Blighty?

Brian   I tend to avoid the cottages.

John   Cottages? Is that the slang? How quaint. Not your scene then? Not a cottager?

Brian   I learnt the hard way.

John   When did you know? That you was –

Brian   A prize catch for the lasses of Liverpool?

John   A homosexual Jew.

Brian   Well, the Jewish element was made desperately clear to me from birth. The homosexual part emerged only slightly more gradually. Much to my daddy's growing dismay. But deep down I suppose I've always known. How long did you suspect it in me before you knew?

John   No offence, Eppy. But you're hardly a hardened Macca.

Brian   Yet still I persevere.

John   When we first met in the Cavern you couldn't keep your peepers off my –

Brian   Not true!

John   And then the band meetings at NEMS. You were trying so hard to maintain eye contact, I thought this fella is deranged. But the sort of deranged that just might nab us a recording contract.

Brian *looks both deeply embarrassed and flattered.* **John** *picks up the bottle of champagne, swigs and passes it to* **Brian***, who tries to resist the urge to wipe the bottleneck.* **Brian** *takes the bottle to the window.*

Brian   You can see the bullring from here. It's one of my favourite things in the world. I want to take you. Terrifying and thrilling all at once.

John *stands nearer to* **Brian***, who moves away.*

Brian   After a while you forget who's chasing who.

John   Handsome, wasn't he? Juanito. From the bar. Muscles in his spit.

Brian   Really? I must have been distracted.

John   You were chatting for almost an hour. Not bad, your dago lingo.

Brian   Neither of us extended any charm beyond common courtesy.

John   But do his charms extend beyond the allure of his arse?

Brian   Here I was thinking you were curious about his potential as an intellectual suitor.

John   I saw you edging closer like a horny little velociraptor. No need to hide your carnal predilections from me, papa Eppy. I've seen exactly how you operate this evening. I understand you completely.

Brian   You wish.

John   I've observed your sensational sinuous snake hips and the deliciously suggestive way you order your tapas. A distinctive flutter of the eyelash. An ever-so-light fey flick of the wrist. There's no getting away from it. You are a sauce pot. Through and through.

Brian (*whispering again, serious*)   Keep your voice down.

John   Juan liked you!

Brian   Juan liked free champagne.

John   Besides the evidence of his massive throbber . . . He literally told me.

Brian   You talked about me?

John   Couldn't stop him rambling on in espaniolay about how much he 'relished your company'. Surely that's fag code for desperate and ready to roger?

Brian   You're really an expert now, are you?

John   Some things I pick up quickly. Girls. Boys. The clap. Number one singles. Small but significant cultural signifiers. (*Donning a limp wrist and popped hip.*) Ain't that so, sister?

Brian   He fancied *you*.

John   Rubbish.

Brian   Asking all sorts of tedious questions. Where did I find you? Did you have a girlfriend? What do you like to –

John   I can tell when you're lying, Eppy.

Brian   That's not what I'm looking for.

John   Surely poofy Peter could be your special friend?

Brian   Peter wants too much.

John   What about that Geoffrey?

Brian   He's too much like me.

John   Oh you like bastards do ya?

Brian   Believe me, I've thought about it night after night, but I just can't see a happy ending to my finding romantic love.

He drinks again. This time a larger swig.

John   Save some for the rest of us, Boozy Brian. Here. (**John** *slips* **Brian** *a couple of pills.*) Might take the edge off.

Brian *meets* **John***'s eyes, then swallows the pills in one go. He passes the bottle back, a little too fast.*

Brian   I wanted to talk to you.

John   What do you think we're doing now?

Brian   The Beatles have been presented with a seriously exciting business opportunity.

John   No shop talk, Eppy. It's party time.

Brian   Parties cost money. Would you like some?

He pulls out a contract from his inside pocket. Places it down.

John   We didn't come all this way just to have the same conversations we have back home.

Brian   How does Cynthia feel about money?

John   Better now we've got a bit.

Brian   Babies are expensive, John.

John   Greedy little blighters.

Brian   Paul mentioned that you –

John   Talk to me before you go scheming with Paul.

Brian   We were only –

John   Understood?

Beat. **Brian** *sits on the bed.*

Brian   Was the tidying up on my account?

John   It's how you prefer it, right?

Brian   I was being sarcastic.

John   You little shit!

Brian   I actually like that you're messy.

John   Because it's manly?

Brian   Because it's you.

John *jumps on the bed next to* **Brian**.

Brian   Does Cynthia enjoy picking up after you?

John   Why we talking about Cyn?

Brian   You must be missing her.

John   There's no need to lay it on like that.

Brian   I was only being polite.

John   Course you were. (*Sighs.*) Missing her or not, I'm here aren't I? You not hot in that suit?

Brian   A little.

John   You always look like you've just stepped out of the bath. Immaculately manicured fingernails. Polite, appreciative, yet commanding, in your dark blue and grey tailored numbers. Made perfectly to measure. Must drive those poor helpless fags wild.

John *swigs.*

Brian   Not the types I'm interested in.

John   Which mythical beasts are strong enough to capture your heart, sirrah?

Brian   The ones that are hard to find and even harder to keep.

John   You think I'm worth keeping?

Brian   What a stupid question.

John *extends the bottle.* **Brian** *tries to take it,* **John** *doesn't let go. Then does. The hotel room phone rings.* **Brian** *throws* **John** *a concerned look.*

John (*nodding to the champagne*)   Second bottle.

Brian (*answering the phone*)   *Dónde está el champán?* Er – (*He stops.*) Oh hello, Cyn.

He looks up at **John** *who signals for him to hang up.* **Brian** *shakes his head.*

Brian (*on the phone*)   How's little Julian doing?

John (*mouthing silently*)   Kipping. Say I'm kipping.

Brian (*on the phone*)   You do sound tired, sweetheart. Are you getting any sleep? Oh John?

John *buries his face in the pillow.*

Brian (*on the phone*)   Of course. He's right here.

John *extends his hand.* **Brian** *places the receiver into it.*

John (*on the phone*)   Hello, little darling. You okay? I was out for a walk. Why would I want to speak to a baby for? He's a baby. Look, Cyn, I'll call you back later, alright? Or tomorrow. Yeah you too. Bub-bye. (*Beat.*) Miss you. (*He hangs up, aggravated.*) You must think I'm a proper bastard.

Brian   Never.

John   A dad for three fucking weeks and here I am on honeymoon. That's how much of a bastard I am. (*Correcting himself.*) Holiday. Fuck, I'm knackered. You know what I mean.

Brian   You need rest. From the baby. From the band.

John   It's not like I had any role models. I've no idea what turns a bastard into a 'dad'.

Brian   Surely it's about encouraging the best in the boy. Allowing Julian to make his own mistakes. Showing him you'll always be there. No matter who or what he becomes.

John   Is that how your pops was with you?

Brian *smiles. Takes a sip.*

John (*off* **Brian**'s *ambivalence*)   Dads are cunts. I've made a mistake, haven't I? Why didn't you tell me I was making a mistake?

Brian   You did the right thing.

John   Why did you really have that flat, Eppy? You'd never mentioned it before. You clearly never lived in it.

Brian   It was meant to be my Spain.

Beat.

John   I want you to be the godfather.

Brian   John, you don't have to –

John   If there's going to be a mini-Beatle in town, he needs a trusty manager. Julian would be lucky to have you looking over him. Cyn won't take no for an answer. He is bloody marvellous, Eppy. Bet you think I'm a soppy git?

Brian   It's very moving to see your passion.

John   That's the difference between 'birds' and 'boys'. I reckon you're more of a 'bird'. That's why I trust you. You'll say yes? For Julian?

Brian   For him and for you.

He toasts **John** *with his glass of champagne.* **John** *picks up the contract from earlier. Begins to read through it.*

John   Everyone thinks we are away fucking all weekend and you're still doing deals.

Brian   Doing deals for you.

John   You shouldn't forget to indulge yourself though. Why should we have all the fun? (*Referencing the contract.*) Merchandise?

Brian   Beatles memorabilia in every shop window around the world. T-shirts. Jackets. Magazines. Dolls even. Little John Lennons with their own miniature guitars.

John   We're not soft-furnishings, Daddy Brian.

Brian   Britain's full of screaming girls all desperate to spend every penny they possess on the 'Fab Four'. It's their heart's ambition to cover every inch of their bedrooms with your faces. People are already selling pillowcases of you in marketplaces. Shouldn't you at least make some money out of your own likeness?

John   We're making money out of music, Eppy.

Brian   Just think how many more fans-to-be will come into contact with your music with exposure like that.

John   The world doesn't need little voodoo dolls of me lurking around in every state from Taiwan to Timbuktu. Besides, I can't trust what you'd do with a doll of me.

Brian   Not just dolls. A fan club.

John   What the fuck is a fan club?

Brian   Handwritten welcome notes from The Beatles themselves and a Christmas disc sent out every year. It's all about making your fans feel part of it all, whilst capitalising on this emerging frenzy.

John   Why would our fans give a fuck about branded-bloody-hankies?

Brian   It's about breaking the mould. Taking things to the next level.

John   We haven't got time for all this, Eppy. We've got albums to make.

Brian   I've been connected to a gentleman who will do it all for us. Nicky Byrne. We'll just sit back and cash the cheques.

John   You trust a guy called Nicky-fucking-Byrne?

Brian   I trust your magnetism. I negotiated the deal. It's a no-brainer. And it'll help our ticket to America.

John   You are obsessed.

Brian   My obsession is to fulfil your wildest dreams.

John   You silver-tongued devil.

John *picks up his guitar. Starts to strum the chords of 'Bad to Me'.*

John   If you're bored – give Cilla a shot.

Brian   I like Cilla. That's why I'm going to help her. But she made a complete hash of it on stage, John.

John   It was my fault. I played the song in the wrong key.

Brian   Timidly spluttering through her lyrics, trembling with stage fright . . .

John   Everyone's falling in love with her down the Cavern. If anyone can make a star of that, it's you.

Brian   You still working on that new song?

John   Maybe. What rhymes with Brian. Besides dying? (*Strums a chord*.) I want to perfect lyrics, not gruesome Sindy dolls. (*Singing*.) There once was a little fag called Bri. He vowed to suck cock until he –

Brian (*singing, big vibrato*)   Makes The Beatles huuuuuugely successfuuuuul!

John   Christ. I know you sang in the choir, Eppy, but you'll never make it as a pop star. You're too posh.

Brian   And you're the bit of rough, Mr Lennon from Walton.

John   Eh, watch your mouth, you. Class is earned. And I worked hard for mine.

Brian   That's no run-down terrace you grew up in.

John   251 Menlove Avenue and proud of it. You know nothing about my troubled youth.

Brian   Did you know I've been commissioned to write an autobiography?

John   At twenty-eight? Impressively young. About all your sordid little affairs?

Brian   About you and the boys. I'm meeting a ghost writer in a few weeks at the Imperial Hotel to 'tell my story'.

John   What's it going to be called?

Brian   We're not certain yet.

John   Don't be shy.

Brian   It's a 'working title' . . .

John   Spit it out.

Brian   'A Cellarful of Noise'.

John   'A Cellarful of Boys', more like.

Brian   We should have gone to Marrakesh or North Africa. We might have at least got some privacy there. What do you think?

John   I think you're a ridiculous little man and I have no idea why people would be interested in your story. 'Queer Jew'! That's what you should call it.

Brian   I knew you'd take the mick.

John *takes off his shirt.* **Brian** *is visibly flustered.*

John   It's scorching, ain't it?

John *kicks off his trousers too. He drinks, then walks around with a peculiar sense of victory.*

Brian   Would you ever write a song about a man?

John   Paul and I sing about each other all the time.

Brian   A love song.

John   Why would I do that? When I have a wife?

Brian   Because it's art.

John   And art is truth.

Brian   Your truth or mine?

John   You'd never let me do it, Eppy. It would be career suicide!

Brian   Not every piece of art is for public consumption.

John   How do you know I haven't already?

Brian *pauses then scoffs slightly.*

John   That's what being an artist is. Experiencing different lives. Different feelings. Impulses.

Brian   You're not just here to gawp at the wildlife?

John   I like spending time with you, Eppy.

Brian   I'm not a tourist exhibit.

John   Brian, I've been trying to fuck you for the last fifteen minutes and all you've done is thrust contracts in my face.

Brian   John, I . . . (*Stunned.*) John.

John   Why the fuck did you get us one bed if you don't want us sharing it?

Brian   I asked for two single beds. They pushed them together.

John   Fuck it then. Let's separate them if you don't want to do owt with me.

He makes to pull the beds apart.

Brian   I can touch you. If you like.

John   Touch?

Brian   And you can touch me.

John   Don't you want to . . .

Brian   Hold you. Be with each other

John   Hold each other? That's a bit queer, ent it?

Brian   Yes. If queer means lovely.

John   You could stick it up my arse. I'm not bothered about being the man.

Brian   Actually, John, I don't really go in for that kind of thing.

John   What's wrong with my arse?

Brian *shrugs. Shakes his head.*

Brian   Nothing.

John   And there's nowt to be scared of.

Brian   Really? This performance doesn't tend to end well back in Liverpool.

John   So the rumours are true? That is where the black eyes come from?

Brian   No good blowjob goes unpunished.

Beat. **John** *fetches the bottle of champagne.*

John   Why don't I let some Juan suck me off and you can watch? Or you can tell him what to do – in your lovely school boy Spanish – and I'll find out what it is when he does it to me.

He gently tips **Brian**'s *head back, feeding him champagne.* **Brian** *drinks obediently. Eyes fixed on* **John**.

John   Look, I know you don't really trust yourself with people. But you can't keep getting beat up and telling yourself that's all you deserve. Let me make this happen for you. You're entitled to a good old-fashioned fucking.

He lets go. Passes **Brian** *the bottle and more pills.*

Brian   I can't. I can't let myself . . .

John *moves over to the merchandising contract.*

John   Fine. I'll sign the tacky thing. (*He signs.*) Are you finally aroused? Are you ready for me? Ready to trust me?

Brian   All I want is to secure your future. Yours, Julian's, Cynthia, the boys. Make all of *you* happy.

John   It's just a shag, Eppy. It's not hard. Yet.

Brian   It's easy to be sexually carefree when you have a wife and child as bona fides. You can pick and choose when you're seen as a man.

John   Can't you see it's dead good to be different?

Brian   Different, maybe. It's the anti-Semitic jibes I could live without.

John   I should put that in a chorus and sing it again and again so people like you would finally hear it.

Brian   Torment us you mean.

John   If you could wake up tomorrow like everybody else, or stay . . . different. Which d'you choose?

Brian   To be like you. Not myself.

John   I would choose to be like you. With that smooth posh voice. And that head full of endless ideas. You are the fifth Beatle. And yet no one recognises you. You can go anywhere you want to go. No one hounding you. No one screaming at you. And as your world expands, my world's getting smaller.

Brian   One jealous twisted fan-girl finds out about me, it would bring down our entire operation. I've been blackmailed before.

John   Have you ever tried sleeping with a woman?

Brian   I couldn't do it to them.

John   Plenty of women would love to ride on your bus, Eppy. You don't need to be exclusively queer. Cynthia has given me so much: consistent love, this feeling of security, a home.

Brian   Then what am I? A drunken bank holiday from your dull but wholesome life?

John   This trip is my last chance to be John from Menlove Avenue. To be really single and flirt with the world. To try new things without it being splashed all over the Sunday papers. They're already making dolls of me. Next comes the pins. I'm about to lose my freedom forever, Eppy. I know you're sad you never really had any. Trust me, you're lucky. 'Cause losing it is shit. And once this is done, I'm heading home to be a shit dad and a shit husband, careening towards an inevitable shit divorce.

Brian   Is this about Cynthia?

John   Don't talk about Cynthia. Ever again. She's a good woman. She don't deserve us talking about her. We don't like the power you hold over us. We've discussed it.

Brian   I only ever think of the band.

John   Making me keep her locked up like a dirty little secret.

Brian   We talked about this . . .

John   It's not nice, Eppy!

Brian   I'm sorry if Cynthia doesn't like the situation. I really am. But to maintain the devotion of teenage girls you must appear attainable.

John   Like you, Rapunzel? Attainable my arse. You want so desperately to be a working-class boy like us. But you never can be. So you torture us by flogging us. Making us presentable to bring home to Daddy. Just like the men you never could.

Brian   You're right. I envy you. And if I had what it takes, I would give anything for one day in your shoes.

John   So you forced me into yours instead? Turned us into emotionless robots that simply strum and twitch on stage.

Brian   I'm not a robot.

John   We were happily feral, wild-haired undisciplined geniuses, and then *you* came along with your master plan saying do this and don't do that. And the most evil thing about becoming exhibits in your cages is we actually became 'successful'.

Brian   If it's so terrible, why are you really here with me then?

John   I told you. Because I'm a bastard. And because you're the only one who has power over me.

Brian   Because it's not enough to be effortlessly sexy and have all the love you crave in the world, you have to have mine. And damn you, that's irresistible.

John   It's not me the girls are chasing. It's not my work that they're in love with. It's yours. I'm what you've made. I was trying for years before meeting you and only got as far as Hamburg. Yeah, I'm a genius, but I'm also nothing.

Brian   But the world is built in your image.

John   The image you've made. I'm yours, Eppy. Don't reject me.

John *starts to cry.* **Brian** *comforts him.*

John   Why is it that whatever I do, I need your approval?

Brian   You already have my approval.

John   You know what I mean. Please, Brian.

Brian   I don't want . . .

John (*kissing* **Brian**'s *shoulder*)   Please, Brian.

Brian   I can't . . .

John (*kissing* **Brian**'s *face*)   Please, Brian.

Brian   Are you doing all of this because you love me or because you hate yourself?

John   We're all driven by something.

He slides closer to **Brian**.

Brian   You really want this?

John   I'm kissing you, aren't I?

Brian *allows himself to be kissed by* **John**. *Slowly, in tandem, they wrap themselves around each other.* **John**'s *earlier chords transform into 'Please Please Me' by The Beatles. Blackout.*

– Interval –

Scene Six

Back in the Cavern Club, now empty and closed. 1963. **Cilla Black** *stands centre stage, rehearsing 'Love of the Loved' with focused energy, her voice carrying through the empty room. In the audience area,* **Brian Epstein** *sits slumped in a chair, watching her with a mix of fatigue and distant admiration, his gaze occasionally wandering. Suddenly,* **Brian** *hears something behind him. He gets up eagerly, hoping for something or someone, but finds nothing. Disappointed,* **Brian** *returns to his seat, slumping back down. At the peak of the song,* **Cilla** *stops mid-line, noticing* **Brian***'s disconnection.*

Cilla   What's going on, Brian?

Brian   Nothing. I'm listening.

Cilla   What were you expecting, then? 'Cause it's sure as hell not me!

Brian   I've got London on the phone twice a day. EMI want another single. The boys want another holiday. Everyone wants something yesterday.

Cilla   And what am I? Still just the cloak girl?

Brian   I could use a friend.

Cilla *softens and steps offstage to sit beside him.*

Cilla   Oh, darling, what's happened?

Brian   Oh just the boys. You know how they are sometimes.

Cilla   They always come back to Daddy eventually.

Brian   There's a lot of pressure is all.

Cilla   You thrive on pressure.

Brian   Pressure's fine. It's the feeling something's about to give way.

Cilla   Then take a holiday.

Brian   I just had one.

Cilla   A proper one. On your bill.

Brian *looks at her, a little surprised, a little uncomfortable.*

Cilla   Your skin's the same pale colour as when you left. I'd be surprised if either of you scallies saw daylight.

Brian   One can get carried away in places like that.

Cilla   Is that right?

Brian   I could stay out there. Not come back. Pack all this in and become a terribly contented Spanish housewife.

Cilla   What about the rest of us? Who believe in you? Who enjoy spending time with you? Who actually want you around?

Brian   You'd get over it.

Cilla   You don't get to quit, Bri. The train's left the station. You said I had something. You're taking me to London. Putting me in front of George-bloody-Martin. That's not a favour. That's a beginning. So how do I deliver?

Brian   Sing the bridge again.

Cilla   That's not what I mean.

Brian   Let's get it perfect first. From the top.

Cilla *stands and gestures playfully.*

Cilla   Did you like how I lifted my arm during that verse, or should I save it for the big finish?

Brian   Forget the arm, love. Nail the key.

He leans back, glancing away.

Cilla   What did he do?

Brian   What are you talking about?

Cilla   Dish it, Brian. I'll find out anyway.

Brian   It's more what he *didn't* do.

Cilla   Which is?

Brian   Nothing. Not a word. Not a call. Not even a row. If John's angry with me . . . If I've misread things . . .

Cilla *gently strokes* **Brian**'s *face, sensing the weight of his words.*

Cilla   He's with his family.

The pain is palpable. **Cilla** *sits on* **Brian**'s *lap, trying to offer comfort.*

Cilla   Y'know, you're my family now. My parents love you enough to let me do this, be here with you. You're not on your own, Bri. Not while I'm around. One day you'll turn on the wireless and it'll be me. And you'll remember – you didn't give up.

Cilla *gently kisses* **Brian** *on the forehead. Instead of being soothed,* **Brian** *begins to gently cry, burying his face to hide it.*

Scene Seven

The sounds of a birthday party spill out onto the quiet Liverpool night, just outside a modest suburban terrace. 1963. The celebration takes a sharp turn as shouts of anger rise above the din, followed by the unmistakable crash of glass breaking. **Cynthia Lennon** *hurriedly drags* **John Lennon** *away from the escalating chaos, her grip firm as the commotion rages behind them.*

John (*shouting offstage*)   Did you enjoy that, you filthy perverted bastard? Did you get off on my fists punching into your ugly leering fucking face?

Cynthia   John! You're going to kill him!

John (*shouting*)   That's what you really wanted, weren't it? Did it turn you on getting smashed up by a so-called fucking shirt-lifter?

Cynthia (*in* **John**'s *face*)   John! Please will you calm the fuck down. They'll 'ave ya for murder!

John   I never liked that sly bastard. Think he can talk shit about me like we're fucking mates? He can fuck off and find a dick to suck if he's so fucking obsessed.

Cynthia   What about your 'mate' Paul? He won't get another twenty-first birthday for you to piss all over. Or another twenty-first birthday cake for you to shower with your other 'mate's blood.

John   Bob-fucking-Wooler is not my fucking mate. Eppy's my fucking mate. That don't make me no queer.

Cynthia   You cannot go around pummelling people for making jokes.

John   This is what those fucking cunts do to people. Talk shite just 'cause folks are different. Try to turn their mates against them. Is Eppy not meant to have any friends? What has Bob ever done for us? Except play our records so he can get girls he can pretend he likes fucking.

Cynthia   Shhh! John please!

John   I'm sorry, Cyn. But I'll swing for any cunt who calls me a fag and I'll die a happy fucking murderer.

Cynthia   Is this how you're planning to teach your son to behave?

John   What? How to stick up for your family? You heard what he said about me and Eppy! (*Off* **Cynthia**'s *face.*) They've been saying it to you, haven't they? (*Grabs her.*) What have they been saying to you?

Cynthia   Ow! You're hurting me!

John   What they been saying to you, Cyn? I'll kill 'em. I'll fucking slaughter anyone who disrespects you.

Cynthia (*hushed rage*)   Don't give me that knight in shining armour bollocks. If you gave a shite about how I feel, you wouldn't have abandoned me and Julian for a bloody holiday! And don't try and sell me that horseshit about you needing to consolidate your influence over Brian and The Beatles' 'business' side of things. You wanted to get pissed up and let loose like you always do. Like we're still seventeen.

John   You told me to go! You said I needed a holiday. You said I was under your feet!

Cynthia   I said what you wanted me to say. Like I always do. You gladly took advantage while I was distracted with Julian.

John   I'm supposed to be the master manipulator now? As well as a mind reader?

Cynthia   I know you're not a fucking mind reader, otherwise you'd be blushing right now. Any husband worth a spit surely knows when his wife needs him. Like, for instance, just after giving birth to his highness's son.

John   Don't be like this, Cyn. You know I can't stand it when you've got a cob on with me. I know my best is the worst, but it's all I've got.

Cynthia   Your 'best'? Is it really your 'best' to spend the rest of our boy's childhood banged up behind bars for manslaughter? Doing your 'best' to derail your entire career? Just as you're finally almost able to provide for you and yours? Wake up to yourself, John Winston Lennon. You've got a woman who loves you. Who is prepared to take everything you can possibly throw at her. No matter what sensational places all this takes you to, or whatever incredible creatures you meet. No matter who tempts you into bed, or tries and fails to steal your hardened heart: they'll never have what we have. What I have. Because I knew you before all of this. I've been committed to you since the moment we first locked eyes and I've not blinked since. Even when what I see really fucking hurts. That's what you've got right here, John. That's what you should be fighting for.

John   I know.

Cynthia   Then fight!

John   There's a line, Cyn. Part of the unspoken code between men. Cross that line and you know you deserve to get your head kicked in.

Cynthia   Since when do you follow rules? You're not a hopeless scally scrapping on the streets of Kirkdale to survive. You're a poncy flamboyant rock and roll singer from Woolton, who went to bloody art school.

John   Urgh. Not you as well, Cyn. Everyone tries to tell me who I am and where I'm from and none of you have a fucking clue.

Cynthia (*smiling*)   Oh aye. Is that right?

John (*smiling a bit*)   Don't dismiss me, Cynthia Lillian Lennon.

Cynthia   People have boring lives. They're hungry for a bit of scandal and a good laugh. Just like you are sometimes. If they're driving you mad, why are you acting like them?

John   I know. I need to sort myself out.

Cynthia   Too fucking right. It's *your* face needs punching in. *You* still make jokes about how Brian is, like it's something to take the piss out of – when he's the best bloody man you've ever known. Done more for you than any bloke has ever bothered to before. Yet you've never defended him till now.

John   I'm not right, Cyn. In the head.

Cynthia   What's changed all of a sudden?

John   Eppy, the poor bastard. He's having a fucking hard enough time anyway. I only went to Spain 'cause I felt sorry for him. He can't help the way he is. Lonely as hell. Never even caught a whiff of what we have. The sort of life we'll share together. Cyn, if you saw what it was like . . . I wouldn't wish his path on my worst enemy.

Cynthia   You wanna be a great artist? You need to think different. Become a different kind of strong. For all of our sakes.

Beat.

Paul's moving to Chelsea isn't he?

John   St John's Wood. With his fancy southern bird.

Cynthia   Let's beat them to it.

John   Really?

Cynthia (*touching him*)   I wouldn't mind being a Kensington lady.

John   Oh yeah? Sipping high teas at Fortnum's and splashing all our moolah down Carnaby Street?

Cynthia   You and Paul will still be neighbours and you can still write songs together in our garden shed. Or Wendy house or whatever they've got down there. (*Embracing* **John**.) Brian will probably move down as well. London's better for him. For all of us. (*Over* **John**'s *shoulder*.) You know . . . if anything did happen with Brian . . . I wouldn't be so fussed. I know what he's like. It'd be different with a woman. But some stupid lark between two mates . . . It's almost sweet, in a way.

John *holds the embrace. Not moving an inch.*

Cynthia   It'd break my heart to find out from someone else.

She pulls away to look at **John**. **John** *holds her gaze, neutrally. Then gently shakes his head.*

Cynthia   Okay. Good.

John   I'll never leave you, Cyn.

Beat.

You know that, right?

Cynthia (*softly, resigned*)   Poor bastard.

John   Who you talking about, Cyn?

Cynthia *sighs. Smiles.*

Cynthia   Let's get you cleaned up.

Scene Eight

We are transported with 'Ritmo de Carmen Amaya' by Carmen Amaya. Atop the music we hear an American radio broadcast recording.

Ed Herlihy (*radio recording*)   Three thousand screaming teenagers are at New York's Kennedy Airport to greet – you guessed it – The Beatles. This rock and roll group have taken over as the kingpins of musical appreciation. New York city cops are hard-pressed protecting The Beatles at their hotel. On every side there is hero worship that recalls the heydays of Elvis Presley and Frank Sinatra. (*Interviewing a fan.*) I understand you're more than ninety miles from home. Are The Beatles really worth all this trouble?

Linda Moore (*radio recording*)   I'd travel a million miles to see my John!

Kimberly Taylor (*radio recording*)   He's not your John! He's that Cynthia chick's.

Linda (*radio recording*)   Try and stop me!

1964. New York City. A lavish suite in the Waldorf Hotel, now a dishevelled aftermath of indulgence – scattered bottles, rumpled sheets and unmistakable signs of recent partying and sex. From the bathroom, the sound of running water mixes with loud, drunken laughter and shouting. **Geoffrey Ellis** *lets himself into the suite, immediately struck by the mess. He surveys the scene, horrified. With no one in sight, his frustration boils over.* **Geoffrey** *marches over to the bathroom door and bangs on it, but the noise inside drowns him out. Exasperated, he pulls a handkerchief from his pocket, kneels, and begins futilely scrubbing muddy footprints from the pale carpet. As he works, his gaze catches on a darker stain* *nearby. He leans closer, curiosity giving way to revulsion. He recoils sharply from the foul aroma, before returning to his task. Suddenly, the bathroom door flies open.* **Brian Epstein** *tumble-runs out, barely wrapped in a hotel dressing gown, laughing uncontrollably. Water sprays from a powerful unseen showerhead, whilst* **Brian** *holds up a small hand towel as if it could somehow shield him from the mess.*

Brian   Cease! Desist, desist! You madman!

Dizz Gillespie (*offstage*)   Submit, motherfuckerrrrrrr!

Brian (*throwing the towel back into the bathroom*)
Never!

Dizz (*turning the shower off*)   Never?

Brian (*shifting inwards*)   I'm sorry, master.

Dizz, *a young American hustler, swaggers out of the bathroom, covered modestly by the small hand-towel.*

Dizz   Okay, pathetic little limey faggot. Face the wall.

Brian *faces the wall.*

Dizz   Spread 'em.

Brian *puts his hands on the wall and adopts a wide stance.*

Dizz (*kicking the inside of* **Brian**'s *legs*)   Wider. (*Leans in, growls into* **Brian**'s *ear.*) Are you ready to meet Uncle Sam?

Brian *moans excitedly.* **Geoffrey** *audibly clears his throat.*

Brian   Hello, Geoffrey.

Dizz (*to* **Brian**)   Don't move!

Brian   What on earth are you doing down there? Have you lost something?

Dizz   Threesomes are double.

Geoffrey (*to* **Brian**)   You're paying for this?

Brian   Trust me, he's worth every cent.

Dizz (*his fingers gripping the back of* **Brian**'s *hair*)
You ain't a-woofin'.

Geoffrey   May I remind you who booked you into this hotel? Whatever sins are herewith committed impact directly upon my reputation.

Brian   Whilst elevating your credibility with the homosexual hotel staff and garlanding you with my sexy rock 'n' roll credentials. Two Jewish boys keeping The Beatles in line. If I can't scandalise the staff on your behalf, what's the point in progress?

Geoffrey   Good Lord. Can you hear yourself? It's 6 a.m., man. The cars are arriving at seven. You've three back-to-back live radio interviews. If you're late, they'll blame the Jews long before they blame the rock 'n' roll.

Brian (*waving some powder*)   Enjoy some magic pixie pick-me-up energy then.

Geoffrey   Party's over, Brian. Time to send the kiddies home.

Dizz (*advancing on* **Geoffrey** *with overwhelming sexual confidence*)   Who you callin' a kid?

Brian   Isn't he thrilling? A real life American he-man.

Dizz (*sniffing* **Geoffrey**)   You smell like a pansy. Makes me mad and hard at the same time.

Geoffrey (*to* **Dizz**)   Have you been paid yet?

Dizz   You think I'm a sucker? I'm Eppy's boyfriend now. Don't get hired without a contract, do you? I'm drawing salary.

Geoffrey   Then piss off until working hours. Your services aren't required.

Dizz   Oh you're really angling for that beat down, huh, princess?

He puts his finger on **Geoffrey**'s *chest and gently but firmly shoves* **Geoffrey** *backwards into an armchair.*

Dizz   You're hard right now, ain't ya?

Geoffrey *doesn't move a muscle.* **Dizz** *settles himself on the chaise lounge. Flicks open his zippo lighter to spark up a smoke. Eyes* **Geoffrey** *with a crooked smirk.*

Geoffrey (*to* **Brian**)   When I was awoken from a deep slumber by a direct call from the Waldorf Hotel's senior manager, I naturally assumed they were calling to complain about high jinks perpetrated by 'the band'. Imagine my horror and mortification on finding out *you* are the disruption. I was then treated to a graphic description of the seemingly endless parade of surly lost-looking gentlemen who were evidently marching directly to and from some mucky construction site, through the lobby, soiling the Axminster that led to your suite. *Mazel tov*, Brian – expect an eye-watering bill on departure.

Brain Epstein   We can afford it.

Geoffrey   One taxi ride later, I find that indeed 'the boys' and Cynthia are all tucked up in bed, exhausted, over-worked and desperately homesick, whilst their formidable impresario is up here feasting with panthers.

Dizz   Those guys are my buddies. Did you see one you liked? We can send a bell boy to fetch him back from 42nd street for ya.

Brain Epstein   Each one was our personal guest.

Geoffrey   Which is exactly what you told the hotel manager, I was reliably informed, whilst writing him a personal cheque in return for his discretion. Is it your ambition to see yourself arrested at the height of your accomplishments? Because I assure you, Brian – I'm helping as a friend, not as your fixer, and my patience is at its limit.

Dizz (*to* **Brian**)   I like this guy. He talks even more fruitier than you.

Brian   Dizz, meet Geoffrey. One of my oldest and dearest friends from grey suburban Liverpool, way back when. The first to flee the dull docks, he's doing a superb job looking after us whilst we're visiting him stateside.

Dizz   Oh yeah? (*To* **Geoffrey**.) Spill. What was baby Brian like as a kid?

Brian   Geoffrey, meet my handsome hunky new beau.

Geoffrey (*to* **Brian**)   You've been outsmarting the world since we were awkward schoolboys. What you've achieved with those lads in three short years – at the enviously sweet age of twenty-nine – is nothing short of a miracle. But I cannot – no, will not – be associated with this madness.

Brian   What are they going to do? You said it. I'm fast becoming one of the most influential men in show business.

Geoffrey   You realise that the authorities would be happy to make an example of you? Particularly with a surname like Epstein. Ever thought about a pseudonym? Disguise things a little? Or is discretion not your forte?

Brian   I'm already 'the Jewish manager'. Even when I'm silent, they still find me 'flashy' or 'pushy'.

Dizz   Fuck discretion. That's for poor folks. We're at the motherfuckin' Waldorf!

Brian   I don't mind if I have to battle with every anti-Semitic arsehole in America. We'll win them all over eventually. We've got Beatlemania. The kids are on side. Right, Dizz? You've heard of The Beatles?

Dizz   Heard of 'em? You're kiddin' right?

Brian   And Dizz was practically homeless.

Dizz   Solid gold hits, baby – every last one!

Brian (*approaching the radio in the hotel room*)
And even after tomorrow's second appearance on Mr Ed
Sullivan's broadcast, (*he dials through the low sci-fi whine of the
a.m. frequency stations*) we still have one more consecutive
Sunday prime-time performance, before our grand booking
at Carnegie Hall. As humble a man as I may be, please allow
me to declare . . . (*He releases the radio dial with a flourish –
echoing the earlier recording, the broadcast brims with excitement
about The Beatles.*) My genius.

Geoffrey   Then why this unfathomable wish to commit
career suicide? I'll be first to confess that I thought your
American master plan would be impossible to pull off. But it
actually worked. Still you're willing to risk everything for a
short-lived teethy blow from one of New York's most well-
attended tourist traps?

Dizz (*laughing*)   You know that's actually pretty funny!

Brian   What's the point in endlessly producing hit record
after hit record, discovering star after star, if I can't enjoy the
salacious spoils of victory?

Geoffrey   The wolves are waiting. Why feed yourself to them?

Dizz *howls like a wolf. Bites at* **Geoffrey**.

Brian   NEMS stands at the forefront of popular
entertainment. I ascertain Elvis's earnings and double them.
We've maximised on merchandise, licensing and publishing.
We're delving into film-making, gracing television screens,
infiltrating the esteemed realms of British theatre, as well as
the authentic atmosphere of the Spanish bullring. There's no
escaping NEMS domination.

Dizz   And little Epstein loves domination.

Geoffrey   Are we really so unshakably certain that all your
deals are 'hits'? (**Geoffrey** *gets out a cigarette, pats his pockets
looking for his lighter.*) Even that 'landmark merchandising
deal' you 'spearheaded' and were so keen for me to look
over?

Dizz *flicks open his lighter, lights it for him.*

Brian   Ten percent royalty on all merchandise sold.

Geoffrey   You do realise, of course, that without The Beatles that company wouldn't be able to make a penny? (*To* **Dizz**.) Thank you. (*To* **Brian**.) Shouldn't the percentage be the other way around?

Brian   Not a finger need be lifted by myself or the boys.

Geoffrey   Fixed royalty with no chance of increase . . . Little to no creative control . . . No way of exiting the contract.

Brian   You fingered through it then?

Geoffrey   You asked me to. Though I'm not entirely sure whether you meant it as a showpiece or a call for help. Either way, I don't work for you, Brian – and that's rather the point.

Dizz (*ruffling his hair down, awful British accent*)
Hey, I'm a Beatle. I'm from down the Pool.

Brian   You fancy being a NEMS star too?

Dizz   NEMS would never survive – too much brilliance in one bloke.

Brian   Mmm. Now call me a mucka.

Dizz *grabs* **Brian** *firmly by the jaw.*

Dizz (*still doing the accent*)   Don't tell me what to do, matey.

Dizz *tosses* **Brian** *away.* **Brian** *rubs his jaw with a mixture of fear, pain and pleasure.* **Dizz** *grabs the powder from earlier and snorts it.*

Dizz (*dodgy British accent*)   That's the ticket.

Geoffrey (*to* **Brian**)   You don't even like that stuff.

Brian *sniffs around for what's left, rubbing the remnants into his gums.* **Geoffrey** *looks away in judgemental disgust.* **Dizz** *balances a pill on the back of his hand.*

Dizz (*to* **Brian**)   Now you're the Beatle.

Brian *snorts the line off* **Dizz***'s hand.*

Dizz (*to* **Brian**)   Sing to me, little bug.

Brian *hums the Jewish lullaby 'Oseh Shalom' very softly. Embarrassed and giggling.* **Dizz** *smacks* **Brian** *round the face with a firm slap.* **Brian** *stops immediately, frozen, not moving an inch.*

Dizz   Pansies blossom in the company of a real red-blooded man. Don't you think, Geoffrey?

Geoffrey *crosses towards the hotel phone.*

Brian (*to* **Dizz**)   Geoffrey's a different kind of pansy.

Geoffrey (*dialling*)   The type that prefers not to court incarceration.

Brian   I'll drink to that. (*Raising his glass.*) Bottoms up!

Geoffrey   You'd never have been so brazen back in Liverpool.

Brian   Why do you think I had to escape? I couldn't bear to be that small any longer. I had to do something so outrageously big. Become so ludicrously successful that all the small town bullshit could be obliterated.

Dizz (*knocking back a drink*)   Boom.

Brian   I know you believe if we are to stand any chance of being 'accepted' we have to prove that we are just the same as all the norms. But fuck it. Who wants to be accepted by the unacceptably unexceptional? Even those who already pretend to tolerate us secretly loathe us the moment we're not designing dresses for them or lacquering their hair or making money for them. And I am making obscene amounts of money for them. So until the day I inevitably fail and they bring out the torches and pitchforks, I can soil any carpet I fucking wish.

He pulls out a handful of dollars, throws them at the stain.
Geoffrey *places the phone back down on its receiver.*

Brian   'Oh dear', you're thinking. 'What happened to good old Brian? We used to be so alike.' Well, we both jumped the fence and escaped the farm. You to the uptight respectability of uptown Manhattan, and I to the quietly flamboyant excesses of rock 'n' roll management. Oh yes, we are still very much alike. I just stopped being appalled by who I really am.

Geoffrey   Really? Somehow that's escaped my notice. Perhaps I'm overtired. (*To* **Dizz.**) It's okay. You can pick them up.

Dizz *begins to pick up the dollars.*

Geoffrey   It's a sin to watch another man suffer.

Dizz   Fuck you. How much is Brian paying *you*?

Geoffrey   When this disastrous transatlantic self-annihilation is finally over, and the Brattles scuttle back to London with what's left of dear Brian, I shall resume my career and put this entire nightmare episode firmly to the back of my hopefully not too permanently damaged psyche.

Dizz   Lemme guess. You work in finance? No, no. You're way too smarmy. You're a fuckin' attorney.

Geoffrey   Insurance lawyer.

Brian   Exceptional at it too.

Dizz (*to* **Geoffrey**)   Wow. You really got daddy Brian eating out of your hand, don't ya? Or is it the other way round?

Brian   It doesn't have to end here, Geoffrey. There's still a desk waiting for you at NEMS.

Dizz (*approaching* **Geoffrey**)   You can touch my body if you like.

Brian (*to* **Geoffrey**)   No one's going to tell on you.

Dizz   I'll even do you a discount. Cause in a fucked up way you're actually kinda hot.

Geoffrey (*to* **Dizz**)   Why don't you look after Brian then, young Sir Dizz the Astute?

Dizz   I plan to.

Geoffrey (*to* **Brian**)   How long can you go on like this? Are you even enjoying it anymore?

Brian   What do you expect me to do? Sit quietly and await my arrest?

Geoffrey   Stop pretending this is freedom.

Brian   I do want to stop.

Geoffrey   Then stop.

Brian   I'm losing myself, Geoffrey. Look at the choices I make, the sort of men I let into my life.

Dizz (*approaching* **Brian** *threateningly*)   Think you're so much better than me, don't ya?

Brian   Anything could happen if you leave me with this scoundrel.

Dizz *grabs* **Brian**'s *arm. Twists it violently.* **Brian** *squeals and grimaces, clearly in a lot of pain.*

Dizz   You think I'm bad? Wait till you see the next son of a bitch.

Brian   I've already been robbed ten times.

Dizz   Maybe the next guy will slit his throat. Maybe I will. If I get drunk enough. High enough. Ashamed enough.

Brian   Aren't you ashamed now? Look at you. Desperate white trash.

Dizz *punches* **Brian** *square in the face.*

Geoffrey   Enough!

He rushes towards **Brian**, **Brian**'s *nose bleeding.*

Geoffrey (*to* **Brian**)   Come with me.

Geoffrey *leads* **Brian** *into the bathroom.*

Geoffrey (*to* **Dizz**)   You're a bloody maniac.

Geoffrey *turns on the tap offstage in the bathroom and begins cleaning* **Brian** *up.*

Dizz (*to himself*)   And you're a good friend. A decent guy. Knew you'd come through.

He counts the dollars he picked up earlier, then his eyes land on something else – a black Samsonite briefcase tucked in the corner. He grins.

(*To himself.*) A gentleman . . . and a treasure trove.

He picks up the briefcase and opens it slightly to inspect the contents – bundles of cash, plenty of pills and personal papers. In a smaller pocket, he finds photographs of nude and semi-nude men.

(*Teasingly.*) Naughty Brian . . . I'm not your one and only, huh?

He shakes his head in mock admiration, slips the briefcase under his arm and heads to the mirror. He tries on the second hotel robe, puffs out his chest and ruffles his hair down again, Beatles style.

(*To himself.*) How you doin', mucka?

The familiar sound of girls screaming quickly descends into boos and aggressive uproar. Chants of 'Ban The Beatles' interspersed with the screaming of 'Go home, Beatles!' and 'Jesus died for you, John Lennon!'. Records are smashed and thrown on to roaring fires. Building to a deafening terrifying crescendo.

Scene Nine

1966. **John Lennon** *and* **Brian Epstein** *are in the studio at Abbey Road. Lit by a red recording light.* **John** *is reading from a handwritten script.* **Brian** *leering impatiently over his shoulder.*

John   Earlier this year, I made a flippant comment referring to –

John *shakes his head and puts the paper down.* **Brian** *lifts it up again. Eyeballs* **John**.

John   I made a flippant comment referring to Christianity, that I neither believed, nor intended to be made public. (*Stopping again.*) Fuck off. I can't do it.

Brian   Just a couple more words . . .

John   This is a bloody farce.

Brian   Just hold your nose, quickly pop it down on tape and then you can fly straight back to your lovely sunny holiday.

John   Did you even read the whole interview?

Brian   Read it? I can't move an inch without seeing your thoughtless verbal diarrhoea blown up in every tabloid newspaper. I hear it discussed endlessly everywhere, by vicars, hairdressers, bartenders and taxi drivers, all around the entire bloody world. Read it?! I can recite your mishap front-to-back, upside-down and in twenty-six different languages.

John   Let's not blow this out of proportion, Eppy.

Brian   Says the man who compared himself to Jesus Christ of Nazareth! People actually want to execute you, John. Violent protests. Radio stations banning your records. Middle Americans burning your albums as effigies. And all you have to do is say a few gentle words to hopefully – please God – end this madness.

John   All these labels. These ideologies. It's not loving.

Brian   And what you said was loving?

John   We're spiritual beings, Brian.

Brian (*sighs*)   John . . .

John   Well, I am. And if you want me to produce works of art then you have to let me express myself, regardless of what society demands I say or do.

Brian   Ah the true master lyricist. Quick set it to music before you're assassinated for heresy.

He pops a pill.

John   Still on the tablets?

Brian *nods to the control booth. The recording light switches off.*

Brian   Think of them as a tribute to your current achievements.

John   Them pills numb you out, Eppy.

Brian   Yet you introduced me to them.

John (*inspecting* **Brian**'s *injured face*)   What happened?

Brian   Closet door. Irony's got a twisted sense of humour.

John   Again?

He steps away from the mic.

Remember New York? If Geoffrey hadn't cleaned up your mess, that sordid suitcase of yours back then, this Jesus furore would look like a Sunday school outing.

Brian   Some minor correspondence and a handful of prescriptions.

John   Love letters and pictures of naked men. Enough to hang you in half the countries we tour. And you're worried about me upsetting a few church ladies.

Brian   I have always given you creative freedom. I keep silent in the studio, if I'm here at all. But when it comes to the business of show – when I actually ask you to do something – you have to know, it's only ever with your best interests at heart. And therefore I strongly recommend you comply.

John   You mean obey?

Brian   Every fucking band in the country is begging me to manage them. And I turn them all down so I can dedicate myself to getting treated like shit by you.

John   Isn't that how you like to be treated? Little Miss Masochism. I assumed you were getting off on all these fucked-up theatrics. Am I wrong?

Brian   And you're not? Let's face it. You're loving all the attention. Now you're too rich and famous to scrap in the streets, you're scrapping in the broadsheets.

John   Ooh, very clever. Should I write that down?

Brian   And the fact that you're risking the boys' lives? Cynthia's? Your child's? Doesn't even cross your onanistic little brain. If you don't give a shit about your own life – or about Paul, who has helped make you one of the most celebrated songwriters in existence – why would you give a shit about the rest of us.

John   So that's what you really think? That if it wasn't for that pretty cunt Paul I'd be dead in the gutter with a pocket full of Irish dirges?

Brian   No. If it wasn't for *me*.

John   Fuck off then and see. Cash in all your chips and bonds and watch what I can do without you.

Peter Brown (*from the control booth*)   Erm, Brian?

Brian   Hmm?

Peter (*control booth*)   Sorry to interrupt.

Peter *enters sheepishly.*

Peter (*to* **Brian**)   Cilla wants to talk to you.

Brian   Tell her I'll call her back.

Peter   You've said that three times.

Brian   Say it a fourth time.

Peter *looks at* **John** *who shrugs.*

Peter   And your mother said to remind you it's Purim.

Brian   Women! Only ever want you when they know they can't have you.

John   I like Cilla.

Peter (*to* **John**)   The offices have switched off all the phones, due to the tidal wave of death threats. Half our staff are too afraid to come to work.

John *nods at* **Peter***, who leaves.* **John** *moves to the mic.*

John (*to* **Brian**)   I'm not doing this for you.

John *nods to the control booth. The recording light comes back on.*

John   I would like to take this moment to wholeheartedly apologise for any hurt or suffering I may have inadvertently caused. The Beatles' music is for everyone, and we hope that you can find it in your hearts to forgive me, so you may enjoy the humble offering of our music once again.

He looks at **Brian** *for validation.* **Brian** *approaches the mic.*

Brian (*to the control booth*)   Erase it.

John   I'm not doing it again!

Brian (*to* **John**)   They're never going to believe that. I wrote it and even I don't believe it.

John   You're taking the piss outta me, Brian Epstein.

Brian   You need to apologise in your own fashion. As a conniving, flirtatious, manipulative, gorgeous scally. Ready?

Beat. **John** *returns to the mic.* **Brian** *gives up a thumbs up to the control booth.*

John   I suppose if I had said television was more popular than Jesus I would have got away with it. I'm not anti-God, anti-Christ or anti-anything. I just said what I said and it was wrong. Or it was taken wrong. I have my own opinions. And I believe God is something in all of us. If you want me to apologise – if that will make you happy – then OK, I'm sorry.

Brian   Perfect.

Recording light goes off.

John   We're not touring anymore.

Brian   Come again?

John   We've decided. Music is what matters. No more endless touring – we concentrate on recording. Get our lives back.

Brian   Impossible!

Peter *enters with* **John**'s *cases.*

Brian   The Beatles need to perform live, John. That's where the music finds its meaning – it's what the fans love you for.

John   They can't even hear us over the screams. And now they're forcing their way in – not for a picture or an autograph – they're taking our actual *shit* from the bog! We're supposed to be the biggest thing in the world, yet here we are, trapped by the very thing that was supposed to set us free. No more, Eppy. This is what's best for the band.

Brian   And what exactly am I supposed to do?

John   We think it's best for you as well.

Peter (*to* **Brian**)   It's not too late to come with us. Swerve the madness and give that brilliant mind a break under the Spanish sun for a day or two. Just like we used to.

Brian   You're throwing it all away. You do realise that?

John *puts on his sunglasses. Takes his cases.*

Brian   You can't spend the rest of your lives idly lounging in the sun. Have you considered what or who funds your bloody holidays?

John   We don't need more money, Eppy.

Brian   There'll be nothing left to pass on to your son.

John   You won't change our minds.

Peter *places a reassuring hand on* **Brian**'s *shoulder.* **Brian** *shrugs it off.*

John (*from the door*)   See you in the studio.

John *leaves,* **Peter** *follows.*

Scene Ten

1967. **Brian Epstein** *is sitting alone in a dressing room, frantically glugging on a hip-flask. On hearing footsteps approaching, he expertly hides the flask away in his suit jacket. Clears his throat.* **Cilla Black** *enters and screams at the sight of him.*

Brian   Cilla, my darling.

Cilla   How on earth did you wrangle yourself back here?!

Brian   There are very few people in this business that don't owe me a favour. But the rumour mill is whispering that you instructed them not to let me in. That's a cruel thing to do to someone who adores you so fulsomely.

Cilla   You're not my manager anymore, Brian.

Brian   So I can't even swing by to support my treasured songbird on this gargantuan occasion?

Cilla   Why change a habit of a lifetime?

Brian   Just two minutes in your hallowed presence, my goddess. Please.

Cilla   Shift ya bum.

Brian *slides over to allow* **Cilla** *to sit on the same chair as him. He drapes himself around her as she touches up her make-up and hair.*

Brian   Look at you. Absolute divinity!

Cilla *ignores him.*

Brian   Two urchins from the streets of the Pool – eternal outsiders. I'm so used to being the only one of anything in a room. And yet here we are, snuggled side-by-side in the star dressing room of your very own titular television show.

Cilla   It's an audition.

Brian   Make no mistake, a screen test is a contract in all but name. I didn't twist half of London's arm to get you in this room for nothing.

Cilla   You never do anything for nothing.

Brian   You and I have achieved more than we could ever have dared dream. How sad to stop now.

Cilla   Sad is definitely the word.

Brian   Just as I've bagged you a Burt Bacharach song for pity's sake. Attached to a huge hit motion picture. Paramount Pictures, darling! America lies prostrate at your sling-backed feet.

Cilla   Some things need to change and I can't change myself.

Brian   You've changed before. Craving another rebrand? My speciality. We can craft you a whole new image. Let's give them something they really won't expect.

Cilla   I like my image. I just wish more people knew about it.

Brian   You're the biggest female star to come out of the north, my lovely.

Cilla   And you're a liability.

Brian   A liability that loves you.

Cilla   Your life is a whirlpool of lavish parties, frequented by showbiz muckers and countless pretty young men. Yet somehow I can't even get you on the blower.

Brian   You can call round anytime. No invitation necessary. You're family!

Cilla   Every time I call you, I get some secretary or, worse, your butler, who's forced to make up an embarrassing excuse before hurrying off the line to mop up your vomit. It's humiliating. And draining.

Brian   That's their function. To help me to support you, at any hour – day or night – the diva requires.

Cilla   You don't call back. You miss meetings. You refuse to visit me.

Brian *reveals a bouquet of flowers.*

Brian   Yet here I am.

Cilla (*exasperated*)   Brian!

She takes the flowers. She inhales their scent then throws them aside.

Cilla   You're driving me insane!

Brian   I've stopped drinking. That's where I've been. Battling the demons in order to better serve my lady.

Cilla   I can smell it on you! Whiskey and desperation.

Brian   What you smell is wish fulfilment and devotion. What you smell, my dear, is love.

Cilla   Love? You don't even treat me half as well as the boys. I know you can't help it, but I deserve more.

Brian   Boys, schmoys. The truth that you're not getting is that you are the *only* girl for me. You're my sister. My daughter. My female twin. My confidante. My precious little songbird.

Cilla   And yet it's always The Beatles first and screw the songbird. Every time. I can't do it, Brian.

Brian   Funny. That's what The Beatles say about you. Every day I have to navigate their tantrums in the labyrinth of envy. And my reward for my unfailing fealty? You're dropping me because – in defence of my clients – I made this one little statement about marijuana.

Cilla   LS-bloody-D! And thanks to your 'one little statement', my ma and da are convinced I've been flinging myself around your living room, arse over tit on the stuff. They don't want me associating with you or with the boys. And on this occasion, I'm finally forced to admit they're right.

Brian   And how am I supposed to manage you without 'associating' with you?

Cilla   Exactly. How?

Brian   You know I had to –

Cilla   – 'protect the boys'.

Brian   They were crucifying Paul as if he's the only one who takes this stuff. When the gentlemen of the press are all on it themselves. It's the sixties. Everyone's experimenting with something. Except you, of course, my admirable angel.

Cilla   You're meant to be a reputable businessman.

Brian   Even more reason to lend my voice to the cause, Cilla. I really believe that pot, marijuana *and even* LSD is all less harmful without question than alcohol.

Cilla *reaches into* **Brian**'s *pocket knowingly. Pulls out the hip-flask.* **Brian** *gently retrieves it.*

Brian   Medicinal brandy, darling. Society's whole attitude to soft drugs is rapidly changing.

Cilla   If you'd step out of your opaque little bubble / for just a moment –

Brian   Ooh opaque!

Cilla   What must your father think? Poor Queenie?

Brian   Ahh yes. The norms. You know, there is a parallel between drugs and so-called 'cardinal sin' of homosexuality. Isn't it silly that we have to wait all this time for the enlightened legislation to go through?

Cilla   Brian, are you listening to me?

Brian   Maybe the Queen will finally change her mind and award me my MBE? That'll please the parents.

Cilla   I know it's not always been easy for you.

Brian   It takes more than a law to change hearts and minds. Just like it'll take more than a few shining stars to change this country's view of us Scousers. You and I both know how they see us, sweetheart. The awkward northern lass and the queer Jew.

Cilla   One day they'll be calling me to the morgue to identify you. I don't want to do it, Brian. I can't.

Brian   If you don't stay with me, you're putting me on the slab yourself. You're the only healthy thing in my life, Pricilla. The Beatles aren't touring anymore. I got bored and fucked them off. All so I could concentrate on *you*.

Cilla (*sighs, trying not to smile*)   Oh, Brian. You are a bad bad boy.

Brian   And you can't resist a bad boy, can you? That's another something we have in common.

There's a knock on the door.

Cilla   One minute!

Brian   Just take me back, Cilla. Why put off the inevitable? What man has ever believed in you this much?

Cilla   Maybe it's better for our friendship, if you and I don't –

Brian   Friendship? Don't insult this epic interconnection between us by dismissing it as a mere friendship.

He takes a swig of the whiskey. Offers it to **Cilla**.

I'll have sex with you. I'll take my clothes off right now. Bare myself before you. You can teach me. Teach me how to love you. (*Undressing.*) Whatever you want. I'm yours, Cilla. Daddy always said we were meant for each other. Always have been and always will be. (*Kissing her.*) I love you. I love you. I love you. I –

Cilla   Put your clothes on, you daft bastard.

Beat. **Brian** *pulls back. Looks* **Cilla** *square in the eyes.*

Brian   I know I'm going to fuck up again. I'm going to come crawling back to you time after time. I know you deserve better. But I will also take us both to a place where we will have a view of the entire universe at our feet.

More knocking.

Brian (*calls out*)   She'll be out when she's ready and not before! (*Turns back to* **Cilla**.) I'm the one, Cilla. I'm your man.

Cilla   I mean it this time. (*Cuts him off before he can speak.*) I don't want you here when I'm done.

She slams the door. **Brian** *freezes, chest heaving. He swallows a handful of pills, hands trembling. Suddenly, a flickering apparition of* **Harry** *appears, gesturing silently, a strange mixture of comfort and judgement.* **Brian** *stretches towards it, hands trembling, but the vision slips away.*

Scene Eleven

1967. **Brian Epstein** *and* **John Lennon** *sit in the back of* **John**'s *psychedelic Rolls-Royce. Parked outside* **Brian**'s *country house at Kingsley Hill, West Sussex.*

John   Fuuuuuuuck! The colours are dancing around in my skull. Fuuuuuuuuuckin' ell! Can you see it, Eppy? It's like every so-called inanimate object in the universe has its own energy – breathing, pulsing, speaking to us in its own weird, special way.

Brian   I couldn't have put it better myself.

John   Where did you get this stuff?

Brian   Peter's new supplier. Don't tell Geoffrey.

John   We have to get the others out here to try this.

Brian   Leave the boys and the wives alone for a minute.

John   Cyn will get a cob on if I'm gone too long.

Brian   Trouble in paradise?

John   Total decimation more like.

Brian   I'd love to help but . . . (*Laughing.*) The door handle is asking me not to touch it.

John   You're fucked.

Brian   You're right.

John   Is that why you fucked up the deal?

Brian   Pardon?

John   The merchandising deal.

Brian   I didn't . . .

John   That's not what the rumours are saying.

Brian   I renegotiated you a more favourable commission.

John   We could've raked in millions when it was all kicking off.

Brian   You wouldn't've even considered merchandise without me!

John   We trusted you.

Brian   You didn't come all the way to Sussex just to berate me?

John   We've got to discuss it sometime.

Brian   I thought all you needed was love? Or was that just for the cameras?

John   Were you too high on drugs? I won't blame you if you were. We probably were too at that point. You're supposed to be the sensible one, daddy Brian.

Brian   And mostly I am. And sometimes I'm the thirty-two-year-old ducker-and-diver from Liverpool doing the very best he can.

John   Thought your dad taught you all about deals?

Brian   Daddy tried to be there for me, in his own difficult way, but no one had ever done what we were doing. Peter was better at securing contraband than contracts. And Geoffrey came along too late to save me from any early misjudgements. I understand it was you boys going out there night after night, but when a deal was particularly tricky, or a business venture faltered, I was the one on the front lines taking all the flak and shrapnel. Make no mistake. I hold myself solely responsible. It's not the loss of money that haunts me the most – though it undoubtedly tortures me – it's the failure.

John   Paul is fuming.

Beat.

I tried to tell him that the merchandising deal was your only major misstep. I mean how could you have known how many dummies of us ugly bastards they could sell? But it cost us big time. Paul just won't drop it.

Brian   Fuck him. I can handle pretty little Pauly.

John   What about his not so pretty little lawyers?

Brian   Paul wouldn't do that to me.

John   No?

Brian   He's living and lording it up inside my country manor as we speak.

John   You know it's not personal, Eppy. What it is is a lot of money.

Brian   What about all the money I've earned for you?

John   I'm giving you a heads-up is all. Paul heard the new Stones' manager got a million and a quarter advance on their new record. He's saying, 'What about us?'

Brian *turns away from* **John**. *Lies back, overwhelmed.*

John   Your contract is coming up.

Beat. **Brian** *doesn't move.*

John   You must be thinking about it?

Brian   I've been thinking about how I've always trusted you. How even with your Aunt Mimi glaring over my shoulder, I wouldn't sign the bloody contract. Even at your most thankless and brattish, you've always been free of me. Yet you'll abandon me now just like that?

John   I'm not saying that –

Brian   I know damn well what you're saying.

John   Fix up or you'll lose us. Simple as that.

Beat. **John** *performs a deep breath in and out, still very high.*

John   Don't shoot the messenger.

Brian   I'll leave that to the Christians.

Both men crack up with laughter.

Brian   Kiss me.

John   No.

Brian   Why not?

John   I don't want to.

Brian   You wanted to once.

John   I had to try it once to see what it was like.

Brian   And the second time?

John   To make sure I didn't like it.

Brian   Sometimes I hate you.

John   Don't say that, Eppy.

Brian   Sometimes I hate you and want you as far away from me as possible. Then I realise that the truth is you're as close to me as anyone can possibly get. (*Points into his head.*) And still I want you closer.

John   You need some water. I'll fetch you some.

John *tries to get out of the car, but topples and falls backwards. They laugh.*

John   Guess you're stuck with me.

Brian   And you me.

John   It's over, you know. With Cyn. I've met someone. Someone alive.

Brian   Of course you have. (**Brian** *tries to smile.*) All I want is a number one hit, every week.

John   You know there's another way to live, don't ya?

Brian   Ahh yes. The Maharishi. And what does the Maharishi say about the love between men?

John   No one can tell you how to live, Eppy, but there are higher states of mind far beyond what you know. And all it takes is sitting on a cushion. Don't you want that, Eppy? To feel real bliss – with your boys?

Beat. **Brian** *thinks for a moment.*

Brian   You really think I can be saved?

The rhythmic pulse of Michael Olatunji's 'Odun De! Odun De!' fills the space. **Brian***, as if overtaken by a feverish trance, swallows a handful of pills and strips off his suit, while the Rolls-Royce and* **John** *fade away. A fleeting image of his father appears again, flickering in and out.* **Brian** *reaches towards it, placing a hand over his heart in a silent, tentative gesture of acknowledgement. His arms lift to the sky, hands raises in ecstatic worship. The rhythm swells, carrying him completely into the moment.*

Scene Twelve

1967. We are inside the sitting room of **Brian Esptein***'s house at Kingsley Hill.* **Brian** *wears a flour-covered apron, atop of some – highly unusual for* **Brian** *– hippy trousers, neck-beads and no footwear.* **Peter Brown** *stands nervously behind him, matching apron covered in dirt, slightly rolled trousers, no shoes.* **Brian** *has a cocktail glass in each hand, as he greets* **Geoffrey Ellis***.*

Brian   Geoffrey, darling! You made it!

Brian *kisses* **Geoffrey** *on both cheeks and hands him a cocktail.*

Brian   We've made your room up for you. Top left for you, Peter to the right. Windows flung wide! Shoes off, for heaven's sake. Feel the timber floors connecting with the soles of your feet. No? We'll get you there. Now, the cook is helping us whip up this terrific recipe – that's tonight's theme; healthy, healthy, healthy! Peter, go fetch some rosemary before we pop the tomatoes in the oven? Actually, I'll do it. Have a seat. Enjoy your mimosa. Rest your weary lallies. Mother will be back in a jiffy. (*From the door.*) Top up in the shaker!

Geoffrey (*to* **Peter**)   How long has he been like this?

Brian (*from the kitchen*)   Or there are juices in the kitchen!

Peter   He's good. He's doing well.

Geoffrey   He looks as though he might explode any moment.

They look out at **Brian** *through the window.*

Peter   I'm aware you and I haven't always seen eye to eye. But I'm enormously grateful to have you here. We've all known each other a very long time. Please, whatever you do, try to stay positive. Fall in line with plans, most will evaporate. Just keep smiling. The scran really does promise to be delightful.

Geoffrey   In other words, buckle up?

We hear **Brian** *bustling from the garden to the kitchen.*

Brian (*from the kitchen*)   Rosemary incoming!

Peter   Grief does strange things to us all.

They hear a crash in the kitchen.

Geoffrey   Indeed.

Brian *enters, invigorated. Removing his gardening gloves. Takes in both his guests, performs a large satisfying sigh.*

Brian   My sisters! My comrades! My best best friends!

He envelopes **Geoffrey** *and* **Peter** *into a tight group hug.*

Brian   I am so *blessed*. I was lying awake last night restlessly ruminating on man's state of loneliness, when suddenly I realised, I'm not lonely at all!

He releases his grip. Pours both men a whisky.

True friends, since the first spasms of awkward adolescence. And the advent of society's demonisation.

He hands them each their glasses. Raises another toast.

Here's to being legal! (*To* **Geoffrey**.) Maybe you'll finally allow yourself some dolly trade from time to time?

Geoffrey   It won't change anything. Not for us. Unless you plan to live your entire life behind closed doors.

Brian   Geoffrey, darling, it changes everything.

Peter (*eyeballing* **Geoffrey** *to back down*)   Here, here!

Brian (*raising a glass*)   To friendship!

Geoffrey *and* **Peter** (*following suit*)   Friendship.

Brian *glugs straight from the bottle.* **Peter** *sips at his glass nervously.* **Geoffrey** *places his drink down to speak.*

Brian   Whilst we've been acquiring our right to exist – however privately – John and the boys stand teetering on the verge of total enlightenment. (*Knocks back another big swig.*) I'm going to see the guru myself after this weekend. You both simply have to come with me. (**Brian** *knocks back a couple of pills.*) The queers need cleansing for our new age. (*Lights up a Marlboro.*) We'll do a couple of practice meditations tonight. (*Takes a drag.*) Then pile into the Bentley and all off to the Maharishi in the morning. What say ye?

Geoffrey   I have to be back in the office first thing Monday morning.

Brian   I'm giving you the week off. Let's chuck work aside and elope to an ashram.

Peter (*to* **Brian**)   I was thinking, Eppy –

Brian   Thinking is spiritual poison.

Peter   – that you and I can rest here until you're ready to return to London. There's really no rush.

Brian   I knew you'd be like this. Both of you struggling to let go of old ways. (*Sighs.*) Which is why I invited some more amenable fellow guests to tip the balance.

Geoffrey   Oh God.

Peter   Who have you invited over, Brian?

Brian   A pair of delicious working boys as your weekend companions. My treat. And also in attendance will be the impressively accomplished and preternaturally comely Mr Simon Napier-Bell, as a prospective suitor for *moi*.

Geoffrey   I thought tonight was about cleansing?

Brian   Trust me, it will be.

Peter   Who is Simon . . . erm?

Brian   Napier-Bell. He's an up-and-coming agent. No reason at all to leech off of me, he's already flying.

Geoffrey   He does sound good for you.

Brian (*to* **Geoffrey**)   You would think that, wouldn't you, Little Miss Suburbia? Marry me off to the first norm, so I'll finally 'settle down' here in sleepy West Sussex. I know you, Geoffrey! I see right through you to the nothingness on the other side.

Peter   Geoffrey was just hoping that tonight was going to be us.

Geoffrey   Brian, we need to talk. (**Peter** *signals* **Geoffrey** *to stop.*) About NEMS. That maniac you've somehow allowed to replace you is driving it all into the ground. Everything we've built together is falling apart.

Brian   Let Sir Stigwood burn it all to ash for all I care. I'm finally free!

The phone rings.

Brian   Do excuse me, gentlemen. (*On the phone.*) Epstein. Oh, Mother! How does it feel to have the house to yourself again?

Peter (*to* **Geoffrey**)   Thank you for setting him off.

Geoffrey (*to* **Peter**)   Me? Why on earth didn't you remove the liquor in the first place?

Peter (*to* **Geoffrey**)   His dad just died, Geoffrey.

Brian (*on the phone*)   We're all at Kingsley Hill now.

Peter (*to* **Geoffrey**)   Now is not the time for him to ride bareback through life.

Brian (*on the phone*)   Have you looked through the paperwork?

Geoffrey (*to* **Peter**)   He needs to get his mind clear and back into work.

Brian (*on the phone*)   There are some delightful properties just down the road from me in London. We'll have you settled in no time.

Peter (*to* **Geoffrey**)   It's work that's driving him to an early grave.

Geoffrey (*to* **Peter**)   No, that's your pills.

Brian (*on the phone*)   You're not listening! (*Mouthing silently to the boys.*) Sorry! (*On the phone.*) You're making me a terrible host, Mother.

Geoffrey (*to* **Peter**)   Work made that man. It'll save him too.

Brian (*on the phone*)   I love you.

Peter (*to* **Geoffrey**)   He's not a machine, Geoffrey.

Brian (*on the phone*)   Goodbye. (*Hangs up.*) What are you two witches gossiping about?

Geoffrey   How is she coping?

Brian   You shan't force me into negativity, Geoffrey! Everything is too amazing to be so glum!

Peter   We're here to listen. If you need to talk.

Brian   Sitting Shiva was such an extraordinary privilege. I really must study the Torah more, it's all in there. I called my rabbi in London and insisted we finally sit down and talk. I think we need to talk to every religious leader. (*To* **Peter**.) Peter, put in a call to the Pope. We can be in Rome by Tuesday. (*To* **Geoffrey**.) He'll meet me now we're legal. The Catholics are all sisters. (*To* **Peter**.) Tell him I've a business strategy for how Jesus can catch up with John, Paul, George and Ringo. (*Laughing*.) If anyone knows it's me! That's why I'm here on the earth. To solve everyone's dilemmas. (*To* **Geoffrey**.) Now Geoffrey, sit. Tell me all about the business.

Geoffrey   Brian. We need to properly discuss the future.

Brian   Discuss what? That you want to polish your halo whilst conspiring to take everything away from me?

Geoffrey   I beg your pardon?

Brian   I've caught you red-handed, Judy Iscariot. You're going to have to try a good deal harder than that to get one over on Eppy!

Geoffrey   Brian, you're handing your precious children over to the carelessness of a money-grabbing outsider. If you wanted an exit strategy, you should have confided in me and we could have devised an effective plan together. Naturally, I always thought that –

Brian   Aha! Truth at last.

Peter (*to* **Geoffrey**)   You?

Geoffrey   It was hardly going to be *you*, was it?

Peter   I'm closest to the boys. They trust me. You're just one of the 'suits' they hate.

Geoffrey   The CEO has to be The Beatles' boss. Not their best friend.

Peter   Maybe I'd be both. Like Eppy always was.

Brian   How deceitful. You two make it look like you want to hang out as friends, but really you want to instigate a hostile takeover.

Geoffrey   Our employees rely on us to feed their families.

Brian   And you'd rather we all just fed you.

Geoffrey   I want to save NEMS for you. For your legacy.

Brian   Liar! You are a cancer and I won't hear another word!

Geoffrey (*to* **Peter**)   You win. I can't deal with this.

The phone rings again. **Brian** *leaps towards it. Signals* **Geoffrey** *to wait.*

Brian (*on the phone*)   Epstein. Simon! How the devil are you?

Peter (*to* **Geoffrey**)   What are you doing?!

Brian (*on the phone*)   Yes, we're all here.

Geoffrey (*to* **Peter**)   Where has your medicated Mother Theresa act gotten us?

Brian (*on the phone*)   We're very much looking forward to receiving you.

Peter (*in hushed rage*)   Where were you when I found him unconscious and unable to wake him? Where were you when I had to make the terrifying decision not to take him to the ozzy, because if the drugs didn't destroy him, the press would?

Brian (*on the phone*)   Speak up, dear, I can't quite make you out?

Peter (*to* **Geoffrey**)   Desperately trying to revive him until the private doctor got there.

Geoffrey (*to* **Peter**)   I was busy stopping the business that pays you from going under.

Peter (*to* **Geoffrey**)   What about our friend who was going under?

Brian (*on the phone*)   Ah. I see.

Peter (*to* **Geoffrey**)   The one who's going under right now?

Brian (*on the phone*)   Of course . . . another time.

Peter *and* **Geoffrey** *exchange a look – they know how this call ends.*

Brian (*on the phone*)   Please procure yourself a marvellous evening all the same, dearest Simon. Bub-bye, handsome man.

He hangs up.

Peter   It's okay, Brian. You have us. We'll look after you.

Geoffrey   You won't find the answer in a man you hardly know.

Peter   We're your best friends, remember?

Brian   You're right. And we still have our other precious cargo en route. I'll put a call in for a third. (*Dials a number.*) The agency will send as many as we want. I am paying them obscene amounts after all. (*Ringing.*) And the chunks will do anything we ask because the customer is *always* right. (**Brian** *slams the phone down.*) No answer. Bitches. (*To* **Geoffrey**.) You really are a sad disappointing case. No wonder the poor Joe Meek slithered into psychosis and shot his silly self – men like you make the world unliveable.

Peter   Geoffrey has always done what you've asked of him, Brian. He's here for you now.

Geoffrey (*to* **Peter**)   Don't speak for me.

Brian   And you, lacklustre Peter, why are you still drooping around after me? You effortlessly enchant any man that sets eyes on you. Yet you insist on pissing all over my heirloom tomatoes.

Geoffrey (*to* **Brian**)   We had to visit you every day at the hospital, Brian. I took you to rehab myself. You listened to the boys' latest 'masterpiece' from a hospital bed, unable to walk. You told us that was your rock bottom. Yet still you search for a lower place to go.

Brian   Making up stories again, Geoffrey?

Geoffrey   Peter found you with a suicide note, Brian.

Brian   Nonsense!

Peter (*to* **Brian**)   It was your will and testament. Leaving your ken, business and dosh to your mother and your brother.

Brian   It would have been for a script or a jape for the boys. You know that I commissioned Joe Orton to write a film for them? He's obsessed with those darker themes. Well, he was. Before his boyfriend bludgeoned him to death. What is it with all this unnecessary dying?

Peter   You're frightened, Brian.

Brian   At least Joe Orton had a lover to kill him.

Peter   There's been a lot of change. But we can help you find your way through this.

Brian   It's fantastic that The Beatles aren't touring any longer. It's even good the merchandising went tits up. It's crass commercialism and blatant capitalism and everything the Maharishi is so very against.

Peter   It must have been a truly difficult day.

Brian (*raising the bottle*)   To being free and unencumbered. (*He drinks.*) You know, for all I've done for youth culture, I've never actually been *young*. (*Another swig.*) When I finally made it to the boys' farewell performance – there had to be probably thirty thousand people – I walked right into the crowd and found myself just screaming like one of the girls. It's what I've always wanted to do from the moment I descended into that fetid basement and clapped eyes on their sweaty quiffs. I've always felt everything a Beatles fan has ever felt. And suddenly, in the heart of it, I just . . .

He screams as loud as he can and for as long as he can. Eventually he stops. Composes himself with a smile.

He loves me.

Geoffrey *and* **Peter** *share a nervous glance.*

Geoffrey (*lightly*)   Who are you talking about, Brian?

Brian   John loves me. He wants to be with me, properly, you see. But we can't. It's not safe. Not yet.

Peter   George, Ringo and Paul love you too. We all do.

Brian   No! Not like I love *John*. Daddy loved John as well. I could tell that he could see what was going on between us. Daddy knew before we did. He was desperate to put a yarmulke on his head and get us married off together. Daddy knew that John was my Queenie. Daddy knew everything.

Peter *and* **Geoffrey** *look at each other again. Worried* **Brian** *has lost his mind.*

Brian   Fuck Harry Epstein and fuck John Lennon.

Geoffrey   Brian.

Brian (*snapping*)   What?

Peter   Take a breather. Count to ten.

Brian   Why don't we go to London? Spend the night in my theatre with that Baldwin fellow? Or we could fly to Spain and watch my Beatle bullfighter in action? Oh and did I tell you that the boys want to buy a Greek island? A whole island. I think it's a dotty idea but they are no longer children and must have their sweet way. Would you like to go to Greece?

Shall I telegraph Onassis? Shall we buy an island? Tell me, dammit, what would you enjoy?

Peter   We're not going anywhere, Brian.

Geoffrey   For heaven's sake, just sit down!

He startles **Brian** *to silence.*

Peter   We'll be calm. Meditate with you. Eat your nutritious meal. Just stay here where we can all be together.

Brian   Only if you pinky swear to stop being such Debbie Downers?

Peter   We'll meditate with you right now. Shoes off, Geoffrey.

Peter *sits on a cushion.* **Geoffrey** *sighs. Takes his shoes off. Sits.*

Peter   Brian. Lead us in the breathing meditation.

Brian *sits. Breathes in and out deeply. Brings his hands to his heart earnestly.*

Brian   Thank you.

He bows to the men.

Thank you for finally hearing me and seeing me as I am.

Beat. **Peter** *bows too. Nudges* **Geoffrey** *to follow.*

Brian   This calls for champagne. (*Leaping to his feet.*) Now kids, no bickering whilst I'm gone. We're back on track now, you hear? No more bitchery!

He flounces through the door.

Geoffrey   It's going to be a long night.

Peter   Who wouldn't want to spend it with Eppy?

Geoffrey   In this state?

Peter   It's a burden to be a quiet messiah. Who can begrudge such a man for taking a short holiday from himself? The least we can do is have the patience to be waiting for him when he returns.

Geoffrey You're still in love with him?

Beat.

(*To* **Peter.**) I'm sorry, dear boy.

The porch light switches on outside the window.

Geoffrey Brian?!

We hear **Brian**'s *car engine turn on.* **Geoffrey** *opens the window.*

Geoffrey (*shouting*) Brian! Stop, man!

Brian's *motor speeds off into the night.*

Geoffrey Fucking liability.

He closes the window.

Peter Hungry? We may as well see what scrans the cook's rustled up.

Geoffrey The problem with believing you're exceptional is that you also believe you're above the things that are proven to work.

Peter You don't think we're exceptional?

Geoffrey Lucky. I think we're the luckiest men alive.

A car pulls up on the drive. **Geoffrey** *peers through the window.*

Geoffrey It's those boys Brian rented.

Peter Bugger!

Geoffrey Quite. They've seen us. What do we do?

Peter We welcome them in. Be the fine hosts Brian would wish us to be. We keep going, as always. Hoping Brian finds his way back to us.

The doorbell rings. **Geoffrey** *opens the door.*

Geoffrey   Welcome. Late? No! You're just in time.

The telephone rings again, its sharp tone reverberating through the space. One by one, other telephones join in, creating a chaotic symphony of distorted, overlapping dial tones. The cacophony swells into a frantic crescendo, a whirlwind of sound, before abruptly cutting to a heavy, ominous disconnect tone.

Epilogue

1967. A memorial service in London.

Cilla Black   The morning Brian Epstein died, I was gobsmacked, didn't have a clue what to do. The first thing in my head was to ring Brian – thought he'd sort it. What do I do, Brian? What do I say? To the press, at the funeral, to meself? How do you tell a world full of strangers that you've lost your best friend? Then it hit me, Brian Epstein was just our mate. Funny, lovely, kind, complicated Brian. Who we let die, on his bill, like . . . Back in that London home he worked so hard for. We hope, bless 'im, it was in a peaceful sleep. (*Beat.*) And there I was . . . am . . . on my bill. No more natterin'. No more rows. No more shared dinners. No more giggles. Just a contract. A very well-negotiated BBC contract – *Cilla*. My first TV series. He'd left it sitting on the bed, right next to where he died. My copy. Waiting for me to sign. His final gift.

Coda

1967. **John Lennon** *is being interviewed by* **Derek Bellis**, *standing outside Maharishi's retreat in Bangor, North Wales.*

Derek   John, we're very sorry to hear about the death of Brian Epstein. Could we get a few words from you?

John   I don't know what to say. We've only just heard, and it's hard to think of things to say. But he was just . . . He was a warm fellow, you know, and it's terrible.

Brian Epstein *appears to* **John**.

Brian (*to* **John**)   My soppy sweet darling boy.

Derek   What are your plans now?

John *turns to* **Derek** *dazed*.

John (*to* **Derek**)   Eh?

Brian (*to* **John**)   Perhaps the world will thank me for finally silencing you for a moment.

John (*to* **Derek**)   We haven't made any, you know. I mean, we've only just heard.

Brian (*to* **John**)   It'll be okay.

John (*to* **Brian**)   You can fuck right off! You bastard! I'm so fucking angry. Was it really an accident or did you top yourself? Or did someone do this to you? Why didn't you bell me? Why didn't you tell me what was really going on?

Brian (*to* **John**)   Stay calm.

John (*to* **Brian**)   You've fucking abandoned me. Just like all the others. If you weren't already dead . . . I'd kill you myself!

Brian (*to* **John**)   I think perhaps you fear you have . . .

Derek   John, where would you be today without Mr Epstein?

John (*to* **Derek**)   I don't know.

Derek   Are you driving down to London tonight?

John (*to* **Brian**)   I keep having this dream that I've been shot. That I'm lying there dead, right alongside ya. Remember that clairvoyant?

Brian (*to* **John**)   Oh you're not still worrying about that nonsense are you?

Derek   You heard the news this afternoon, I believe?

Brian (*to* **John**)   You're not like me. I had to go. Whereas you're just beginning.

Derek   And Paul's already gone down?

Brian (*to* **John**)   You'll live forever, John.

Derek   You've no idea what your plans are for tomorrow?

Brian (*to* **John**)   Timeless.

John   No.

Brian (*to* **John**)   More than a star. A living legend.

John (*to* **Derek**)   We'll just go and find out, y'know. Just have to play everything by ear.

Brian *is overwhelmed by grief. Trying desperately not to show it.*

Brian (*to* **John**)   You do realise of course you are my greatest achievement?

Derek   I understand that Mr Epstein was to be initiated here tomorrow.

John   Yes.

Brian   It makes me proud that my name will forever be associated with yours.

Derek   I understand that this afternoon Maharishi conferred with you all. Could I ask you what advice he offered you?

John   He told us . . . Uh . . . Not to get overwhelmed by grief.

Brian   We're a team. You and I.

John   And whatever thoughts we have of Brian to keep them happy.

Brian   As are you and Paul.

John   Because any thoughts we have of him will travel to him wherever he is.

Brian   As will you and Yoko.

He smiles. Touches **John**.

Derek   Had he ever met Mr Epstein?

John   No. But he was looking forward to meeting him.

Brian   My darling boy.

Derek   Have you a tribute you would like to pay to Mr Epstein?

Brian   Ours is a great love story.

John   Well, you know . . . We don't know what to say.

Brian   Will you play for me?

John   We loved him and he was one of us.

Brian   Please. Please please me?

John   You can't pay tribute in words.

Brian   I always love to hear you play.

A guitar appears. Or something magical. **John** *plays a new song. Sings. Soft, hopeful. As he sings, the private moment swells, blurring into a gig – the roar, the scale, the phenomenon.* **Brian** *watches from the wings. He begins to sing along. Blackout.*

Discover. Read. Listen. Watch.

A NEW WAY TO ENGAGE WITH PLAYS

This award-winning digital library features over 3,000 playtexts, 400 audio plays, 300 hours of video and 360 scholarly books.

Playtexts published by Methuen Drama, The Arden Shakespeare, Faber & Faber, Playwrights Canada Press, Aurora Metro Books and Nick Hern Books.

Audio Plays from L.A. Theatre Works featuring classic and modern works from the oeuvres of leading American playwrights.

Video collections including films of live performances from the RSC, The Globe and The National Theatre, as well as acting masterclasses and BBC feature films and documentaries.

FIND OUT MORE:
www.dramaonlinelibrary.com • @dramaonlinelib

For a complete listing of
Methuen Drama titles, visit:
www.bloomsbury.com/drama

Follow us on X and keep up to date with
our news and publications
@MethuenDrama